THE GROWING RUSSIAN MILITARY THREAT IN EUROPE

HEARING

BEFORE THE

COMMISSION ON SECURITY AND COOPERATION IN EUROPE

ONE HUNDRED FIFTEENTH CONGRESS

FIRST SESSION

MAY 17, 2017

Printed for the use of the
Commission on Security and Cooperation in Europe

[CSCE 115–1–2]

Available via www.csce.gov

U.S. GOVERNMENT PUBLISHING OFFICE

25–605 PDF   WASHINGTON : 2017

For sale by the Superintendent of Documents, U.S. Government Publishing Office
Internet: bookstore.gpo.gov   Phone: toll free (866) 512–1800; DC area (202) 512–1800
Fax: (202) 512–2104   Mail: Stop IDCC, Washington, DC 20402–0001

THE GROWING RUSSIAN MILITARY THREAT IN EUROPE

COMMISSIONERS

WITNESSES

[III]

APPENDICES

THE GROWING RUSSIAN MILITARY THREAT IN EUROPE

May 17, 2017

COMMISSION ON SECURITY AND COOPERATION IN EUROPE

WASHINGTON, DC

The hearing was held at 9:30 a.m. in Room 208-209, Senate Visitors Center (SVC), Washington, DC, Hon. Roger F. Wicker, Chairman, Commission on Security and Cooperation in Europe, presiding.

Commissioners present: Hon. Roger F. Wicker, Chairman, Commission on Security and Cooperation in Europe; Hon. Christopher H. Smith, Co-Chairman, Commission on Security and Cooperation in Europe; Hon. Sheldon Whitehouse, Commissioner, Commission on Security and Cooperation in Europe; Hon. Jeanne Shaheen, Commissioner, Commission on Security and Cooperation in Europe; Hon. Robert Aderholt, Commissioner, Commission on Security and Cooperation in Europe; Hon. Cory Gardner, Commissioner, Commission on Security and Cooperation in Europe; Hon. Marco Rubio, Commissioner, Commission on Security and Cooperation in Europe; and Hon. Benjamin L. Cardin, Ranking Member, Commission on Security and Cooperation in Europe.

Witnesses present: Dr. Michael Carpenter, Senior Director, Penn Biden Center for Diplomacy and Global Engagement; Stephen Rademaker, Principal, The Podesta Group; and Ambassador Steven Pifer, Senior Fellow and Director of the Arms Control and Non-Proliferation Initiative, The Brookings Institution.

HON. ROGER WICKER, CHAIRMAN, COMMISSION ON SECURITY AND COOPERATION IN EUROPE

Mr. WICKER. Good morning to everyone. Our first hearing on April 26th rightly focused on human rights abuses within Russia. Today's hearing will examine Russia's actions beyond its borders, specifically Moscow's use of military force to further its ambitions. The mandate of the Helsinki Commission requires us to monitor the acts of the signatories, which reflect compliance with or violation of the articles of the Final Act of the Conference on Security and Cooperation in Europe, also known as the Helsinki Final Act.

Even a casual observer of international affairs would recognize that Russian military aggression has posed a tremendous threat to the European security in recent years. The Russian leadership has chosen an antagonistic stance, both regionally and globally, as it seeks to reassert its influence from a bygone era. The actions taken by the Russian leadership under the aggressive posture of Vladimir

(1)

Putin have, without any doubt, violated commitments enshrined in the Helsinki Final Act and other agreements.

To name three examples: Number one, Russia has breached its commitment to refrain from the threat or use of force against other states. Number two, Russia has breached its commitment to refrain from violating their sovereignty, territorial integrity, or other political independence. And third, Russia has breached its commitment to respect other states' right to choose their own security alliances. Many of Russia's neighbors have faced Russian military aggression in recent years. Ukraine and Georgia have both seen important parts of their territories forcibly occupied, including the illegal attempted annexation of Crimea in 2014.

Russian forces continue to be present in Ukraine, Georgia and Moldova, against the wishes of the governments of those countries. In addition to its direct aggression toward its neighbors, Moscow has also made it a priority to undermine the effective functioning of several conventional arms control agreements and measures for confidence and security building.

These measures, to which Russia is a party, include the treaty on conventional armed forces in Europe, which limits heavy ground and air weapons in Europe and provides information on current arms holdings, including their location. Number two, the Open Skies Treaty, which provides for mutual unarmed aerial reconnaissance of member states. And, number three, the Vienna document on confidence and security-building measures, which provides for information exchanges, on-site inspections, and notifications of the military activities, arms, and force levels of OSCE-participating states. These agreements, along with others such as the INF Treaty—which Russia is also violating—together form an interlocking web of commitments that have proved fundamental to the stability of the post-Cold War European security architecture. They were designed to enhance military transparency and predictability, thereby increasing confidence among the OSCE-participating states. Unfortunately, the actions of the Russian leadership in recent years have demonstrated that it sees little value in the transparency and predictability that have kept the peace in Europe.

I want to reiterate my dismay regarding the tragic death of American paramedic Joseph Stone on April 23rd. Mr. Stone, of Arizona, age 36, was killed while serving his country as a member of the OSCE Special Monitoring Mission in Ukraine when his vehicle struck an explosive, likely a landmine, in separatist-controlled territory, an event that also injured two other monitors. This is the first time in history of the OSCE that a mission member has been killed in the line of duty.

And make no mistake, Mr. Stone's death was directly related to Russia's aggression toward its neighbors. Had Russia not invaded Ukraine, and had it lived up to the Minsk Agreement and ceased supporting, directing, funding and fueling separatists in this region, there would have been no need for the monitoring mission to continue. So I once again extend my condolences to Mr. Stone's family, including his son, and his many friends. I want to take this opportunity to call for an end to the harassment faced by these brave monitors on a daily basis. And I urge all sides to provide the observers with unfettered access. We have put a photograph to my right, over my shoulder, of OSCE monitors as a reminder of the continuing challenges faced by these brave monitors as they carry out their extremely important mission.

Our hearing today will have three objectives. First, examine Russia's undermining of European security, the OSCE and its arms control agreements and commitments. Secondly, assess whether it will be possible to move Russia back toward compliance. And third and finally, explore how we can maximize the value of our agreements in the OSCE as a whole going forward.

I'm grateful to the members of our distinguished panel for their willingness to provide expert views on these topics. And I look forward to our discussion today. We'll first hear from Dr. Michael Carpenter, now a senior director at the Biden Center for Diplomacy and Global Engagement at the University of Pennsylvania. Next we will hear from Stephen Rademaker, who has previously testified on a number of occasions before our Commission. Mr. Rademaker is a former assistant secretary of state who headed three bureaus in the State Department. And thirdly, we will welcome back Ambassador Steven Pifer, who has appeared before the Commission previously. The ambassador currently serves as the director of the Arms Control and Nonproliferation Initiative at the Brookings Institution.

We're joined by my friend, Congressman Chris Smith of New Jersey. Congressman, would you have some opening remarks before we hear our testimony?

HON. CHRISTOPHER H. SMITH, CO-CHAIRMAN, COMMISSION ON SECURITY AND COOPERATION IN EUROPE

Mr. SMITH. I do. Thank you very much. Thank you for convening this very important hearing to examine Russian military aggression in the OSCE region. Russia today stands in violation of the central commitments of the Helsinki Final Act. These commitments include respect for the territorial integrity of states, fundamental freedoms, and the fulfillment in good faith of obligations under international law. In violating these commitments, Russia is threatening the foundations of European security and recklessly endangering the lives of millions.

One such victim, that you just mentioned so well, is Joseph Stone, the 36-year-old American medic who was killed by a landmine while on patrol in separatist-controlled eastern Ukraine with the OSCE's Special Monitoring Mission. And he lost his life on April 23rd. If it wasn't for Russia's aggression, and the plethora of challenges that they faced from the beginning of that deployment, there would have been no death of that wonderful young man, Joseph Stone, and so many others—about 10,000 lives that have been lost in this conflict.

Russian aggression is not a localized phenomenon. It threatens the entire region. Moscow has seized sovereign territory by force, threatened to use tactical nuclear weapons against other countries, harassed U.S. and allied military assets, and abandoned key transparency measures and commitments. These actions are unacceptable. In the face of such provocations, the United States must leave no doubt that we stand behind our Eastern European and Baltic allies. There is no time to waste. We must ensure the confidence of our friends at this critical juncture.

One way to do this is to continue building a credible conventional deterrent to Russian aggression alongside our allies, in particular Poland and the Baltic States. I and many others have consistently supported robust funding for the European Reassurance Initiative. With the support of this initiative, since 2014 NATO members have held over 1,000 military exercises in Europe. ERI has allowed the U.S. to participate more extensively in such exercises and increase its deployment of soldiers and military assets in allied countries.

Furthermore, it has also helped us to build the capacity of our partners and generally make our commitment to European security felt. These kinds of activities must be sustained and expanded to ensure that we are ready to counter any threat at any time. This hearing will give us an opportunity to learn what more the U.S. can do on this front, both bilaterally and within NATO.

In particular, I look forward to Dr. Carpenter's testimony about the extent of the challenge posed by Russian aggression in the OSCE region; Secretary Rademaker's thoughts about the implications of Russia's flouting of its arms control and transparency commitments; and Ambassador Pifer's perspective on developments in Ukraine and what they mean for the region. Again, thank you, Chairman, for convening this important hearing.

Mr. WICKER. Thank you very much.

And welcome to all of our guests today. We'll begin with the testimony of Dr. Carpenter. Thank you, sir.

DR. MICHAEL CARPENTER, SENIOR DIRECTOR, PENN BIDEN CENTER FOR DIPLOMACY AND GLOBAL ENGAGEMENT

Dr. CARPENTER. Chairman Wicker, Co-Chairman Smith, Commissioner Whitehouse, thank you for this opportunity to speak to you today about the Russian military threat to Europe. There is no question that the Putin regime today poses the greatest threat to the security of Europe, and to the United States. Over the last decade, the Kremlin has twice used military force to violate borders and occupy other countries' territory. It has breached arms control agreements, such as the CFE, INF and Open Skies Treaties. It has undermined transparency and confidence-building measures, like the Vienna Document. And it signs political agreements that it never intends to honor, such as the 2008 Georgia ceasefire and the Minsk Agreements on Ukraine.

One of the chief drivers of Russia's aggression, and its deliberate violation of international agreements, is its desire to roll back Western influence in the post-Soviet region by subverting the foundations of Western democracy and undermining NATO and the EU. In the non-NATO countries, Russia has proven it is willing to use military force to achieve its aims. In NATO countries, it is turning to asymmetric tactics, such as cyberattacks, covert subversion operations, and information warfare. In either case, denial and deception, unpredictability, and non-transparency maximize Russia's advantages. Nuclear threats and dangerous military activities are also meant to send a deliberate message to the West to stay out of Russia's neighborhood.

In other words, Russia's dangerous and unpredictable behavior is part of a deliberate strategy. Whereas Russian foreign policy for much of the last 25 years was based on cooperating with the West where possible and competing only where necessary, now Russia is engaged in a full-blown competition short of conflict across all domains all the time. That is why is not the time to negotiate new European security arrangements or agreements with Russia. Expanding channels of crisis communication is important and necessary. The administration should also consider a new round of bilateral strategic stability talks to clear up faulty assumptions that could lead to miscalculation. But in general, we have to understand that Russia is no longer interested in cooperation to strengthen European security—just the opposite.

Our goal, therefore, should be to continue to bolster defense and deterrence in Europe. The U.S. should consider suspending its compliance with the NATO–Russian Founding Act so long as Russia continues to violate its basic principles. This would allow the U.S. to permanently deploy an additional brigade combat team to Eastern Europe as a deterrent force, a step that could be reversed if and when Russia's aggressive posture in the region changes.

The United States should also employ the legal principle of countermeasures to respond to Russia's violations of the Open Skies and INF treaties. Just as Russia denies access to part of its territory under the Open Skies Treaty, the United States should restrict Russian access to U.S. territory until Moscow returns to compliance. The same is true of the INF treaty. The United States should immediately begin research, which is legally permitted by the treaty, into the development of an intermediate-range missile that would match Russia's new capability. And the Pentagon should be tasked with implementing more robust defensive measures to deny Russia an advantage in the meantime.

With regards to Ukraine, Congress should encourage the administration to lift the existing de facto arms embargo and provide defensive armaments such as air defense, anti-tank and counter-artillery capabilities. The United States must also get off the sidelines and join France and Germany in the Normandy Group negotiations to develop a road map with concrete timelines for implementing the steps laid out in the Minsk Agreements. It is clear that Russia is not going to honor its commitments until greater leverage is applied.

One option is to inform Russia that sanctions on Russian banks will go into effect if Russia fails to honor specific deadlines for implementing the Minsk road map. The U.S. can do this unilaterally since, unlike sanctions on the defense or energy sectors, financial sanctions can be highly effective even if the EU does not match them. The administration should also consider developing the mandate for an armed U.N. mission for eastern Ukraine.

In response to the cyberattacks and information warfare that the Kremlin has perpetrated against the U.S. and our European allies, the U.S. should invest significantly more resources in cyber defense. And Congress should legislate a common set of cyber defense standards for the private sector companies that control our critical infrastructure. We are way behind the curve on this.

Finally, we must immediately appoint an independent special prosecutor to determine whether or not there was collusion or cooperation between the Russian Government and Trump campaign representatives in the last election cycle. Congress must also establish a select committee to look at the broader question of Russian interference in the U.S. electoral process and Russia's ability to undermine our institutions and infrastructure.

Chairman Wicker, Co-Chairman Smith, members of the Commission, the United States has an obligation to enhance deterrence and build resilience against Russian aggression and malign influence across the OSCE region. It starts here at home, by responding forcefully to Russia's subversive actions. We must also push back on Russia's violations of arms control and confidence-building agreements. And finally, we must apply greater leverage against Moscow, and strengthen Ukraine's defenses. If we do not check Russian aggression with more forceful measures now, we will end up dealing with many more crises and conflicts, spending billions of dollars more on the defense of our European allies, and potentially seeing our vision of a Europe whole and free undermined. Thank you and I look forward to your questions.

Mr. WICKER. Thank you, Dr. Carpenter.

Mr. Rademaker.

MR. STEPHEN RADEMAKER, PRINCIPAL, PODESTA GROUP

Mr. RADEMAKER. Thank you, Chairman Wicker, Co-Chairman Smith, Commissioner Whitehouse. Thank you for the invitation to testify today. Let me say at the outset that I work at a government relations firm in Washington. We have a number of clients. I'm not here on behalf of any of my clients. I'm here on behalf of myself. I was asked to present my personal views, and that's what I'm doing here.

I was asked to assess Russia's compliance with the various arms control agreements that Chairman Wicker outlined in his opening statement. I have prepared a lengthy written statement. I will summarize the written statement and then come to my conclusions.

The first treaty I was asked to evaluate in terms of Russia's compliance was the CFE Treaty, Conventional Armed Forces in Europe Treaty, that was concluded in 1990. This was a very important treaty. The conventional military imbalance in Europe, the advantage that the Soviet Union and the Warsaw Pact had during the Cold War was the driver of the nuclear arms race for much of the last century. And with the achievement of the Conventional Armed Forces in Europe Treaty, the imbalance was corrected, and it became possible to negotiate deep reductions in nuclear force levels. And so this was a very important treaty at the time it was concluded.

Regrettably, in 2007 President Putin ordered what he called a suspension of Russian implementation of the treaty. Now, this is not something that the United States or any of our allies consider to be a legally permissible step on their part. It's essentially breach of the treaty by Russia. We have continued to try to implement the treaty to the extent we can. But in 2011, we and our allies concluded that Russia was determined not to comply. And so we have stopped requesting inspections and expecting data declaration by

Russia pursuant to the treaty, although among ourselves we continue to abide by the CFE Treaty. And technically we hold that it's still in force.

The reason that Russia essentially pulled out of the CFE Treaty in 2007 was because for a long time Russia had become increasingly unhappy with the way that the treaty applied to them. Russia was especially unhappy with what are called the flank limits of the treaty, which limited military deployments on Russia's periphery. They believed that those limits interfered with their ability to prosecute the war they were waging in Chechnya, for example.

They were also very unhappy that the treaty was being used by Georgia and Moldova to try and compel Russia to withdraw its armed forces from their territory. Those armed forces remain present in those two countries without the consent of the two governments. And that is a violation of the CFE Treaty. Those countries, with our support, were pressing Russia to withdraw those forces, and to eliminate the equipment that Russia had deployed in those countries. For all of these reasons, Russia reached the conclusion in 2007 that this treaty no longer served their interests. And as I indicated, President Putin suspended Russian implementation of it.

The second treaty I was asked to look at was the Open Skies Treaty. This unarmed aerial observation treaty is a confidence-building measure. There are 34 parties to it among the OSCE countries. Russia continues to implement the Open Skies Treaty, but it does so in a way to minimize the benefits of the treaty to other parties, such as the United States.

Perhaps the best illustration of that is the Kaliningrad Oblast, which is that part of Russia that's sandwiched between Poland and Lithuania. It doesn't border the rest of Russia. Obviously, it's a very sensitive piece of territory. It's subject to aerial observation under the Open Skies Treaty. Russia has adopted, unilaterally, restrictions on the overflights that would be conducted for surveillance purposes. The effect of these restrictions—they limit the distance of the flights out of the relevant airfield in Russia. The effect of that restriction is not to prevent us from doing aerial observation of Kaliningrad, but it requires us to use multiple flights to completely observe the territory of the Kaliningrad Oblast. So it's essentially a nuisance restriction designed to make it harder for us to achieve the benefits under the treaty to which we and our allies are entitled.

They've adopted a number of other measures—minimum altitude restrictions that limit observation over Moscow. They've previously applied that same restriction over Chechnya. They ended that last year. But again, they were trying to minimize the benefits of this treaty to us with respect to Chechnya. They do not allow flights adjacent to Abkhazia and South Ossetia, those two regions of Georgia. And then in the case of Ukraine they've adopted a nuisance restriction. They require Ukraine to make payment in advance before Ukraine can conduct overflights over Russian territory. This is inconsistent with the provisions of the treaty. And the consequence has been that Ukraine has not conducted any overflights of Russia since that policy was adopted. So Russia implements the treaty, but it does so in a way designed to defeat some of the purposes of the treaty.

Similarly, I was asked to look at the Vienna Document, which is what's called a CSBM, a confidence and security-building measure about force levels in Europe. And Russia has implemented it in a very similar manner to the way that it has implemented the Open Skies Treaty. They comply with it, but in a way that minimizes the benefits. The State Department's annual arms control compliance report, which it issued just last month, said the following, which I think said it all about Russian compliance with the Vienna Document. The State Department said: "The United States assesses that the Russian Federation's ... selective implementation of certain provisions of the Vienna Document, and the resultant loss of transparency about Russian military activities has limited the effectiveness of the CSBM's regime. Russia's selective implementation also raises concern as to Russia's adherence to the Vienna Document."

As with Open Skies, there are a number of examples of things they've done to not fully implement their obligations under the treaty. Perhaps the best illustration or the best example is with regard to advanced notification of military exercises. A pattern has emerged where Russia either provides no advanced notification or notifies that there will be a limited exercise, and then when the exercise takes places it turns out to be a much larger exercise. They put forward legal explanations for this. Sometimes they claim that, you know, these were just snap exercises, or they claim that these were multiple exercises under separate command and therefore they didn't have to be notified as one exercise. But considering the pattern, these are sort of legalisms, and they really reveal a pattern of attempting to minimize their compliance with their commitments under the Vienna Document.

Finally, I looked at the INF Treaty, a very important treaty that limited intermediate-range missiles in the United States and Russia, where both countries are prohibited to have these missiles. Under the Obama Administration, it was determined that Russia was testing a missile that was not compliant with the INF Treaty. More recently, it's been reported in the press that Russia has moved from testing that missile to actually deploying it. And it's supposed to be operationally deployed with two Russian battalions.

Both the Obama Administration and the Trump Administration have tried to have a dialogue with Russia about this to persuade them to correct the violation. It's a very sterile dialogue, because the Russian side essentially says, we have no idea what you're talking about. There is no such missile. We've never tested such a missile. The U.S. government has presented details about the location of—you know, geographic coordinates of tests, the dates of tests. The Russians throw up their hands and say, we have no idea what you're talking about. There was no such test.

So there's not even really a willingness on the part of the Russians to engage in a dialogue about returning to compliance. The underlying issue here, I believe, is that, as with the CFE Treaty, Russia concluded some time ago that the INF Treaty no longer serves its interests. I think they consider it's an unfair treaty because it prohibits them, and us, to have intermediate-range ballistic missiles and cruise missiles. But it doesn't impose such a restriction on some of Russia's neighbors—like China, Iran, Pakistan, North Korea. And those countries are deploying missiles of those ranges. So from Russia's point of view this is unfair to them. And for a long time, they've expressed interest in trying to get out from under the treaty. I think their steps to simply deploy a missile that violates the treaty is consistent with their view that they need to somehow sidestep the restrictions of the treaty.

So my conclusion is that, looking at the overall pattern of Russian compliance with their arms control agreements, that Russia will comply with them to the degree that Russia judges that they serve Russia's interests. But to the degree Russia concludes that these treaties and transparency measures no longer serve its interests, it will either seek to terminate them, as it did with the CFE Treaty; it will violate them, while continuing to pay lip service to them, as it's doing with the INF Treaty; or it will selectively implement them, as it is doing with the Open Skies and Vienna Document agreements.

So what's the underlying issue here, both with respect to arms control and some of the other activity we see in Ukraine, for example? What I suggest in my concluding remarks in my testimony is that, regrettably, Russia sees security in Europe as a zero-sum game. And it thinks the best way to enhance its security is by diminishing the security of its neighbors. And that, of course, is completely inconsistent with the OSCE principles and the principles that underlie all of these arms control and transparency agreements. Because the principle that underlies them is quite the opposite, that security in Europe is a positive-sum game, that all countries will be more secure to the extent their neighbors are more secure.

I think the evidence we have, of course, is that Russia just takes a different view of that, and thinks its security is enhanced if a country like Ukraine's security has been diminished. And I think until we can change that fundamental mindset—and I don't know that we can change that fundamental mindset. It may just be a matter of time and experience that gets us to a different place with Russia. But until Russia stops thinking of the European Union as a threat, and NATO as a threat, and strong and stable neighbors as a threat, and rather sees that as a net positive for their own security, I think we will continue to see these problems in compliance with arms control treaties and similar problems that we have in other areas.

Thank you.

Mr. WICKER. Thank you, Mr. Rademaker.

Ambassador Pifer.

AMB. STEVEN PIFER, SENIOR FELLOW AND DIRECTOR OF THE ARMS CONTROL AND NON-PROLIFERATION INITIATIVE, THE BROOKINGS INSTITUTION

Amb. PIFER. Mr. Chairman, Co-Chairman Smith, members of the Commission, thank you for the opportunity to appear today to testify on the Russian military threat in Europe and how that threat has manifested itself in Ukraine. I will summarize my statement for the record.

Russian actions towards Ukraine have grossly violated fundamental principles of the Helsinki Final Act, including the commitment of the participating states to respect each other's sovereignty, territorial integrity and independence, and to refrain from the threat or use of force. It is useful to understand Russian end goals as regards Europe and Ukraine. Moscow seeks a sphere of influence in the post-Soviet space. It wants to weaken NATO and the European Union.

President Putin and the Kremlin, moreover, appear to fear the prospect of a modern, successful democratic Ukrainian state. The fear is that that kind of Ukraine could prompt Russians to question why they cannot have a more democratic system of governance.

In February 2014, after then-President Yanukovych fled Kiev, Ukraine's Parliament appointed an acting president and an acting prime minister who made it clear that Ukraine's number one foreign policy goal was to draw closer to the European Union. The Kremlin apparently concluded that it lacked the soft power tools to prevent that. Shortly thereafter, the Russian military seized Crimea. Within days, following a sham referendum, Russia annexed Crimea. In April 2014, Russia began assisting armed separatism in the eastern Ukraine region of the Donbas, providing leadership, financing, ammunition, heavy weapons, other supplies, and, when necessary, regular units of the Russian army.

Three years of fighting, despite the Minsk II Agreement worked out in February of 2015, have resulted in nearly 10,000 dead. Unfortunately, the ceasefire and withdrawal of heavy weapons from the line of contact that were called for under the Minsk II Agreement have not been implemented. While Moscow implausibly denies involvement in the Donbas, NATO and Ukrainian officials believe that Russian military officers continue to provide command and control, training and advising for forces there. The Kremlin is not pursuing a settlement of the conflict, but instead seeks to use a simmering conflict as a means to pressure and destabilize the government in Kiev.

The Organization for Security and Cooperation in Europe has played an important role in trying to find a solution to the conflict, chairing a trilateral contact group that brings together Ukrainian and Russian officials, as well as representatives of the occupied part of the Donbas. OSCE also has a special monitoring mission on the ground in Ukraine, with some 700 monitors, many of them who are observing the implementation or non-implementation of the Minsk II ceasefire and withdrawal provisions. And it was that mission that Mr. Joseph Stone was a part of.

What is needed to bring peace, however, is a change in the Kremlin's policy. The United States and the West should support Kiev politically and, provided that the Ukrainian Government more effectively implements economic reforms and anticorruption measures, give Ukraine additional economic assistance. The United States should continue to provide military support, and that should include certain types of lethal assistance such as man-portable anti-armor weapons. The United States and the European Union should continue to put political and economic pressure on the Kremlin. That means keeping in place the economic and other sanctions on Russia. And the West should consider applying additional sanctions.

In addition, it is important that the administration and NATO continue the steps agreed at least year's NATO summit in Warsaw, to enhance the alliance's conventional deterrence and defense capabilities in the Baltic region and Central Europe. Such steps will lead to more secure European allies who will be more confident in supporting Ukraine. The United States should also continue to support the German and French efforts to promote a solution to the Ukraine-Russia conflict. It is very difficult to see Minsk II succeeding, but it is the only process on the table.

At the end of the day, Ukraine needs a settlement which has Russian buy-in. Otherwise, Moscow has too many levers that it can use to make life difficult for Kiev, and thereby deny Ukraine a return to normalcy.

Finally, it is all but impossible to imagine Russia agreeing to return Crimea. At present, Kiev lacks the leverage to change that. The United States and the West, however, should not accept this. They should continue a policy of non-recognition of Crimea's illegal annexation, and continue to apply sanctions related to the peninsula.

Mr. Chairman, Co-Chairman Smith, members of the Commission, over the past three years Russia has employed military force to seize Crimea, and sustain a bloody armed conflict in the Donbas in pursuit of the Kremlin's goal of asserting a sphere of influence and frustrating the ability of Ukraine to succeed. These Russian actions are in stark violation of Moscow's commitments under the Helsinki Final Act and other agreements. These actions endanger peace and stability in Europe. They raise concern that the Kremlin might be tempted to use military force elsewhere.

The United States should work with its European partners to respond in a serious way. That will require a sustained and patient effort, but it is essential if we wish to see the kind of Europe that was envisaged when the Final Act was signed in 1975. Thank you for your attention.

Mr. WICKER. Ambassador, you say that the Minsk II Agreement is not likely to be abided by, but it's all we've got. Dr. Carpenter suggests that any type of an agreement—new agreement or negotiation with Russia is pointless. Help us understand, is there daylight between the two of you there? I'll start with Dr. Carpenter first.

Dr. CARPENTER. I'm not sure, Senator, that there's all that much disagreement between Steve and myself. I agree that Minsk provides right now the only road map that is bought into by all the parties that are concerned, including France and Germany, with this conflict. My point simply is that Minsk—and this is where I agree with Steve—will never be implemented until we apply greater leverage on Russia.

So until Russia feels there are consequences, and until we identify concrete timelines under which the various steps that are laid out in the Minsk II Agreement, the February 15 agreement—unless there are timelines and consequences for failing to meet those timelines, Russia will continue to engage in these Kabuki negotiations with the French and Germans, which are, frankly, going nowhere.

Mr. WICKER. Mr. Ambassador?

Amb. PIFER. I would agree. The first problem in implementing Minsk is that the Russians do not want it to be implemented. There is no doubt in my mind that with Russian control of their forces, but also over separatist forces in the occupied parts of Donetsk and Luhansk, if Russia wanted to deliver a ceasefire and withdraw the forces from the line of contact and allow the OSCE monitors full access, those are the first three provisions of Minsk II. The Russians could make that happen. It hasn't happened now in two years and two months because the Russians do not want it to happen.

There's an additional problem, though, and this is why I think we need to have a sense of urgency about Minsk. The longer that we go since the year 2015, it becomes harder, I believe, for the Ukrainian Government to implement some of the political provisions, such as passing a constitutional amendment on decentralization, or passing a special status law, because you have public attitudes and attitudes within the Rada, Ukraine's Parliament, which are hardening, because over two years they see more and more Ukrainian dead. But Minsk II, right now it's the only process. We need to do what we can to push it. But it's going to require pressure on Russia to change the Kremlin's calculation.

Mr. WICKER. Mr. Ambassador, you mentioned success in Ukraine. Would you and Dr. Carpenter help us by defining success? And isn't that success one of the most important foreign policy achievements we could assist with?

Amb. PIFER. I believe a successful Ukraine is important for the kind of Europe that we want to see—that's a Europe that's stable, secure and at peace. It is going to be a problem that the United States Government cannot ignore if you have a failing Ukrainian state on the border of institutional Europe. That's going to be a problem that is going to be something that we will have to deal with. On the other hand, if you could see a successful Ukraine— and by success, I mean, a normal democracy, a growing market economy, a country that increasingly looks like, say, Poland, its neighbor to the West, that would be success.

The problem that the Ukrainians have is the Russians, I believe, fear that kind of success, because they worry that the Russian population will say, well, wait, the Ukrainians, who the Russians see as probably the closest of the post-Soviet peoples—the Russians start asking, how come the Ukrainians can have a democracy or they can vote, or they have a political voice and we can't? That disturbs the Kremlin.

Mr. WICKER. But, Dr. Carpenter, in spite of all of the problems, if we saw that success, it would be a major achievement for the West, would it not?

Dr. CARPENTER. I agree, Senator, that Ukraine is pivotal to the future of European security. And if the Kremlin looks 10 years from now on its military intervention—violating borders and annexing territory, occupying another chunk of territory—as a success on its part, then that will just fan the flames of Russian ambition, revanchism across the whole region, and we will continue to deal with these sorts of crises in the future. So I think strengthening Ukraine's sovereignty through empowering its reformers, but also hardening its defenses, is absolutely vital.

And just one other point on this. I think Russia would be happy to settle the conflict peacefully. But what Russia's vision of the Minsk II settlement looks like is where you create an analogous situation to Republika Srpska in Bosnia for the Donbas. In other words, they have a veto over foreign policy. They can, in fact, veto a lot of other policies that pertain to the national state. And that would give Moscow leverage to prevent Ukraine from moving towards NATO or the EU for the indefinite future. But that is not success for us. For us, success has to be a sovereign, independent Ukraine that develops on its own trajectory, and hopefully one that is increasingly democratic.

Mr. WICKER. The Republika Srpska example is certain one that we would want to avoid.

We'll continue with six-minute rounds. Mr. Smith.

Mr. SMITH. Thank you very much, Mr. Chairman.

Let me just say, thank you very much, all three of our distinguished witnesses, for their very incisive comments. It really does help this Commission, and I think by extension both the House and the Senate, to have the benefit of your insights. So thank you so very, very much.

Let me just ask, Mr. Ambassador, you pointed out in your testimony that it's important that the United States continue to provide military assistance. You make the point that in particular man-portable anti-armor weapons, to increase Ukrainians' ability to deal with the influx of Russian armor in the Donbas, is one of the points that you underscore. And my question would be from the beginning—because, you know, many of us have been frustrated almost to tears in our inability for years to provide the kind of deterrence capability to the Ukrainians to end the fighting. Without a credible threat of deterrence—as Poroshenko told us in a joint session of Congress, you can't fight a war with blankets. Blankets are important. Medicine is important. But you've got to have deterrence. Have we done enough in the years to date? And is there any sense that you have that we are now looking at a pivot where we will now give them the capabilities to deter so that negotiations can be successfully concluded?

Amb. PIFER. Well, yes, sir. I think that's an excellent question. I do not believe the United States has provided what it could to Ukraine. I was in Kiev and also at the Ukrainian field headquarters in Kramatorsk in Donetsk about two years ago, along with one of my successors, Ambassador John Herbst, and also retired General Chuck Wald, who'd been the deputy commander of the U.S. forces in Europe. And what we heard from the Ukrainians at Kramatorsk was that some of the non-lethal assistance was very useful in terms of, for example, counter-battery radars. But they pointed out that their stocks of Soviet-era man-portable anti-tank weapons just didn't work. So that was a huge need. And they cited that in view of increasing armor that they saw the Russians bringing in to equip separatist forces in the Donbas. So I think that would be a very important need.

I would also make the point that I believe that all three of us came away from our conversations both in Kiev and Kramatorsk believing the Ukrainian army understands they cannot beat the Russian army. They're not talking about give us weapons to drive the Russians out of Donbas. What they want is, they want weapons that allow them to raise the cost to the Russians of further aggression, to take away easy military options—which I believe is in our interest in terms of steering the Kremlin away from military solutions towards a genuine political settlement.

Mr. SMITH. Let me ask Mr. Rademaker, with regards to arms control, is there any penalty for Russia's violations of its commitments, solemnly entered into and at the time we thought faithfully entered into? And have the Iranians, close friends and allies of Russia, gleaned any lessons? Because I'm one of those who believes—and I'm not alone; there's Democrats and Republicans who believe the Iranian deal was egregiously flawed, and we believe it's already, with regards to ballistic missiles, when they kept that out of the treaty—or it's not even a treaty, the executive agreement—will violate with impunity at the time and place of their of their choosing. I'm talking about Tehran now. But did they learn something from the Russians? And, again, is there any penalty for violating any of these arms control treaties?

Mr. RADEMAKER. Thank you, Co-Chairman Smith. Your question really goes to the issue of the limits of arms control. Arms control is a consensual process. Countries sign arms control agreements because they decide it's in their interest to do so. But treaties, agreements, they're governed by international law. And under international law, treaties can be terminated. And that's important, actually, for getting countries to sign treaties in the first place, because if it were seen as an irrevocable step, lots of countries would hold off signing treaties. So we have to take the good with the bad. The fact that countries who sign arms control agreements know that they can get out of them is part of what contributes to their willingness to enter into the process.

But it also means that countries who over time conclude that a treaty is no longer serving their interest have the legal option of getting out from under it. I think President Putin would consider that that's what he did in the case of the CFE Treaty, with this suspension of Russian implementation. They didn't formally terminate Russian participation, but they've suspended it. The effect is essentially the same. You know, Russia's no longer complying. If we really push the issue—the legal issue, I guess what we end up with is a notice of termination and a notice of withdrawal from the treaty by Russia. I think there's still some hope that maybe Russia will have a change of heart. They've never been really pushed on the question of, well, why don't you just terminate the treaty, rather than suspend your implementation.

In the case of INF, I think the Russian position is that they're complying with the treaty, and that these allegations that they have tested and now deployed a non-compliant cruise missile are fantasy—fake news, I think is what they would say about that. The U.S., I believe, is pretty confident in its intelligence information about these tests. There's a mechanism for dialogue under the treaty, where the parties of the treaty can come together and talk about compliance issues.

But it's not like we can take them to court—there's no panel out there to adjudicate disagreements. We have the option of terminating the treaty. I think some are wondering whether we should do that. I personally do not favor termination of the INF Treaty, because I think that would actually be a gift to Russia. I think Russia would like us to terminate the treaty. And I think we ought to be looking at ways to punish them for cheating, not doing things that they would consider a reward for cheating on the treaty.

Dr. Carpenter laid out some ideas about what we should be doing in a case like the INF Treaty. I think taking steps to show that we are prepared to respond, that we will potentially develop and, if necessary, deploy our own missiles that correspond to the ones that they're deploying, looking at enhancements in our missile defense capabilities to counter the illegal missiles that are being deployed on the Russian side. Those kinds of steps are perfectly appropriate and those are the things that we should be doing. But at the end of the day, we can take reciprocal steps in response to what they do, but if we really push the issue then they can withdraw from these treaties.

As far as the lessons that Iran could take from that—in other venues I've testified in opposition to the Iran nuclear deal for some of the reasons you alluded to in your question. I think it's too good a deal for Iran over the long term. It enables them to achieve nuclear weapons threshold capability and then, at a time and place of their choosing, they can deploy nuclear weapons. Now, that's prohibited under the Nuclear Nonproliferation Treaty. But, you know, North Korea was part of the Nuclear Nonproliferation Treaty until they decided they didn't want to be anymore. And now they have nuclear weapons. So I think there's a takeaway for the Iranians from that experience.

Mr. WICKER. Thank you, Congressman Smith.

Senator Whitehouse.

HON. SHELDON WHITEHOUSE, COMMISSIONER, COMMISSION ON SECURITY AND COOPERATION IN EUROPE

Mr. WHITEHOUSE. Thank you, Chairman.

Dr. Carpenter mentioned the array of non-kinetic tools that Russia uses—cyberattacks, covert political subversion and information warfare, and described Russia's intensity on them as all domains, all the time. The CSIS Kremlin playbook looks at this same pattern of activity and draws what I think is a very reasonable conclusion, which is that corruption is at the heart of all of those techniques and is ultimately the enabler of a great many of those techniques, which causes me to wonder whether we have done enough as the United States of America to take on the vast international infrastructure of corruption enablement that the Panama Papers gave us one little window into.

But it's a much broader world of people who are paid a lot of money—lawyers, accountants, and others—to take care of kleptocrats, hide their money, allow super-wealthy people to dodge taxes, and, of course, enable corruption. It seems to me that with the EU cleaning up its incorporation transparency, America now looks to be the last bastion of shell corporations and that that is a significant vulnerability against this larger context. And to the extent that our political money is not transparent at all, that's a vector for foreign influence as well as whatever special interests now take advantage of the dark money operations.

I guess my question is, from zero to 100—with zero being we're doing nothing and 100 being we've really got this—how far along the spectrum do you all feel we are in terms of knocking down the infrastructure of corruption enablement and closing up the vectors of corruption that the United States presents?

Dr. CARPENTER. Thank you for that question, Senator. I completely agree that the name of the game right now for Moscow is the weaponization of corruption to be able to subvert Western societies and Western liberal democracies. In terms of where we are on the spectrum——

Mr. WHITEHOUSE. And just to jump in one point on that—but please continue—but these non-rule-of-law corrupt countries actually need rule of law when it comes to hiding their assets, because if they leave them in Russia they'll get scooped by Putin or the next bigger thug that comes down the road. So they're in an interesting balance where they actually depend on rule-of-law countries to enable their corruption even though they are operating outside of rule of law, I believe.

Dr. CARPENTER. I think that's absolutely right. I think that in terms of where we are on the spectrum, I think we're in the single digits. We're just beginning to come to terms with the threat and how it's manifested. Russia's using a variety of different tools. It's using our media freedom to sow disinformation through various Russian outlets, but also through social media bots and trolls. It's using political pluralism to be able to covertly fund parties, candidates, think tanks, NGOs. We see this across Europe. And then it's using also oligarchs and business ties to be able to subvert and corrupt economic interests in foreign countries that can then be used to lobby for political outcomes. So it's across the board.

I think, for us, Citizens United allows for a vast amount of money to flow into our party financing system with very little transparency and accountability. And clearly, Russia—perhaps other states as well—have taken advantage of that. I would recommend the creation, actually, of an interagency taskforce between law enforcement, between the intelligence community, the State Department and the Pentagon to look at how to root out Russian organized crime networks, and also these organized crime networks are also usually coterminous with some of these corrupt influence operations.

Mr. WHITEHOUSE. My time has pretty well run out, but if I could get the other two witnesses to give me a number on that zero to 100. Michael thinks we're in single digits on those fronts.

Amb. PIFER. Way below where we should be. I can't quantify it. But when I was in Ukraine——

Mr. WHITEHOUSE. Way below. And—I don't want to go into my colleagues' time. Mr. Rademaker.

Mr. RADEMAKER. I'll agree with Ambassador Pifer. Way below where we should be.

Mr. WHITEHOUSE. OK.

Thanks, Chairman.

Mr. WICKER. Thank you, Senator Whitehouse.

Senator Shaheen, and then Congressman Aderholt.

HON. JEANNE SHAHEEN, COMMISSIONER, COMMISSION ON SECURITY AND COOPERATION IN EUROPE

Mrs. SHAHEEN. Well, thank you all very much for being here. And I want to follow up on the measures that we can take to put more pressure on Russia in Ukraine. You talked about lethal weapons as being one of those. I know that shortly—as the Minsk Agreement was being negotiated there was reluctance from the Germans and the French to provide lethal weapons. Has that changed? Anyone, do you know?

Dr. CARPENTER. I can start. There was reluctance from a lot of our West European allies to provide lethal weapons to Ukraine. Now, when Chancellor Merkel first raised this in February of 2015, when essentially the media had gotten wind of the fact that there was some debate here about the possibility of providing lethal weapons, her statement was not unequivocal. She said that it would not be beneficial at that moment in time, but it was not unequivocal.

I personally believe there are a lot of our NATO allies, especially on the eastern flank of the alliance, that would welcome U.S. leadership in this regard and that, in fact, would follow suit rather quickly after we were able to provide lethal weapons in providing weapons of their own. And for Ukraine, this is actually very important because a lot of these former Warsaw-backed allies have non-NATO standard equipment, that is the type of equipment that the Ukrainian military is most used to using and currently employs and would benefit from, because their stocks have been radically depleted over the course of the last two and a half years of war.

Mrs. SHAHEEN. Does anybody disagree with that?

Amb. PIFER. I would just briefly second Mike's point. And note that when we were at NATO two years ago, we heard from certain allies that, yes, if the United States did that, that would give them political cover to also begin providing lethal assistance.

Mrs. SHAHEEN. I would just point out that I know the Armed Services Committee in the Senate has taken a position—general the majority of us—in support of that. I'm not sure about the Foreign Relations Committee. But this is one area where the United States could exercise some leadership and add to the pressure on Russia.

Sanctions is another area. Do we have any sense of whether the Europeans are going to support rolling over those sanctions again, to continue to put pressure on Russia?

Dr. CARPENTER. Senator, I would say right now there is a good chance that the Europeans will roll over sanctions. I think it would be very difficult for them to apply any additional sanctions above and beyond what's been applied right now. My suggestion for the United States to be able to apply greater leverage is to focus on financial sanctions because the defense sector and the energy sector sanctions can easily be backfilled by both European countries, but also by Asian—Korea, Japan, Singapore and other countries that have expertise in this area. On the other hand, financial sanctions are primarily dependent on the U.S. dollar and the U.S. financial system. So we could easily crank up the financial sanctions on a calibrated ladder, and have great effect in terms of the impact on Russia's economy in the near term.

Mrs. SHAHEEN. And I assume you all are probably familiar with the more comprehensive sanctions bill that has been introduced. Is that the kind of sanctions effort that you think would be helpful? Or are you not familiar enough with the bill to be able to——

Dr. CARPENTER. No, I am familiar with Senator Cardin and Senator Corker's collaboration on this bill.

Mrs. SHAHEEN. I'm actually talking about Senator McCain and Senator Cardin.

Dr. CARPENTER. Oh, the McCain bill. I think it's a step in the right direction. It is not tied to specific benchmarks for implementing Minsk. I would suggest that that would be a way to incentivize better behavior by the Russians. But generally speaking, I support that bill.

Mrs. SHAHEEN. Mmm hmm.

Amb. PIFER. And I would just add, I would hope that the bill would also, though, would make it clear that if the Russians met those benchmarks that the sanctions would come off. I mean, that's been, I think, a problem in the past sometimes with Congressional sanctions, is that they go on. But if the Russians can't see a possibility that those sanctions will then come off when the Russians deliver the desired behavior, the sanctions lose their value as inducements to better behavior by the Kremlin.

Mrs. SHAHEEN. And one other question; I know the Magnitsky legislation actually put sanctions on individuals—so prevented certain individuals from coming to this country. How effective are those kinds of efforts in addressing some of the corruption issues that Senator Whitehouse and you all were talking about, and also in trying to ratchet up pressure on Putin and his allies in Russia?

Dr. CARPENTER. I believe, Senator, that those sanctions are highly effective, and precisely for the reasons that Senator Whitehouse indicated, that a lot of these oligarchs have money stashed in Western countries. The thing about the Magnitsky legislation is that it has been vastly underutilized by both the previous administration and this administration. There are only a couple dozen, as far as I know, individuals that have been sanctioned under that legislation. And largely, it is targeted at a narrow group of people around Putin. If it were more widely applied to target those who are corrupt and who violate human rights within the Russian system, it would have a significant impact.

Mrs. SHAHEEN. And don't you agree that we should also include the families of some of those individuals, that we should not allow some oligarch to corrupt countries and send his kids to our universities to get the best education they can, to go back and be part of these networks?

Amb. PIFER. I think that would be a fantastic way to increase the pressure on the oligarchs. If the kids cannot go to the United States or Britain to go to college, and spouses can't travel to do their London or Paris shopping trips, that increases the pressure.

And I think we should be looking at ways to put pressure on the Russians to stop what's going on in Eastern Ukraine.

Mrs. SHAHEEN. Absolutely. Do I still have any time?

Mr. WICKER. You'll have time later. [Laughter.] But very helpful suggestions. Thank you, Senator Shaheen.

Congressman Aderholt, and then Senator Gardner.

HON. ROBERT B. ADERHOLT, COMMISSIONER, COMMISSION ON SECURITY AND COOPERATION IN EUROPE

Mr. ADERHOLT. Thank you. I apologize for coming in a little late. There were a lot of meetings, as you can imagine, here in the middle of the week here on Capitol Hill. But I did want to just talk a little bit about Russia's political leadership, how they are appearing to build a modernization of their military, and of course we're getting reports of that, that they are now ranked right there, overtaking Saudi Arabia and now ranked behind U.S. and China. And I'd open this up to anybody—any of you on the panel here What are the main elements of Russia's military modernization program that you're aware of and that you're seeing right now?

Dr. CARPENTER. Well, I can start. Russia's military modernization was launched when Putin came to power in 2000—really, in earnest around 2005. They've had over a decade in which they've been at this. They have both reorganized their military to be more agile in terms of the structure—it's focused on brigades now as opposed to divisions.

But they've invested heavily and are investing in modernizing their nuclear triad. They have superb, world-class nuclear-powered submarines that have very quiet acoustic signatures that are very difficult to detect by U.S. submarine watchers—either undersea or also in the air. They have developed world-class cruise missiles, as we saw, the ones that were fired from the Caspian Sea and the eastern Med in the Syrian theater. And they have exceptional cyber and electronic warfare capabilities, which we have seen as well in Ukraine and in Syria. And their air defense systems are not as good as ours, but they're pretty good and they're pretty powerful. So, across the board, they've invested significantly in military modernization.

Just one caveat here. A lot has been made of their A2/AD, anti-access, area-denial capabilities. These are very sophisticated capabilities, but sometimes these are little bit overblown. I think the U.S. has the capability, both through standoff munitions—either air launched or sea launched—to penetrate some of the A2/AD bubbles. So, while they do have a significant capability there, it's perhaps been hyped up a little bit too much in recent months.

Mr. RADEMAKER. In the case of their modernization in the strategic nuclear area, I think it's largely driven by Russia's perception that there's a conventional military imbalance in Europe really across their periphery, to their disadvantage. And so in some ways it's the mirror image of the Cold War situation, where we and NATO were satisfied that there was a conventional imbalance in favor of the Warsaw Pact and in favor of the Soviet Union. And we had to rely on nuclear weapons, a nuclear deterrent to ensure the security of Europe.

I think since the end of the Cold War, the Russians have been convinced that the opposite's true, that they're at a conventional military disadvantage. And so their doctrine relies increasingly on both strategic nuclear weapons and also tactical nuclear weapons. And you see investments by them in this area that I think underscore that they believe that nuclear weapons really are the last guarantor of their security.

Amb. PIFER. Congressman, I tend to worry less about what the Russians are doing in terms of strategic nuclear modernization because a lot of it is replacing old stuff with new stuff, as we'll be doing in about 10 years' time. And their modernization program seems to be sized to fit within the limits of the New START treaty. I tend to worry much more, though, about what they're doing in terms of tactical nuclear modernization, and things like this "escalate to deescalate" doctrine which suggests that they may have a threshold for nuclear use that is much lower than would be wise.

Mr. ADERHOLT. It's the same for you all as far as your major concerns. Thanks for mentioning your concerns. That was my next question, what would be your—Dr. Carpenter—what stands out as the most concerning to you about particular aspects of these build-ups?

Dr. CARPENTER. Well, I think the conventional military buildups are a concern. As we've seen in Ukraine, the multiple rocket launch systems and the artillery that is slightly older in terms of the technology have been highly lethal. It has decimated the armored personnel carriers that have been used by the Ukrainians on the battlefield. And we see similar in Syria. And so for our partners and our allies, this is a huge concern—less so in the event of a conflict with the United States. But then we're talking about a strategic confrontation, which is an entirely different ball game.

I am concerned as well about the "escalate to deescalate" doctrine for settling a conventional conflict. This is a doctrine that allows for Russia to use a nuclear weapon first in the conflict to try to terminate it on Moscow's terms. And you can envisage the use of a tactical nuclear weapon, potentially a very low-yield tactical nuclear weapon, which would be potentially highly escalatory. And so this may be an aspect of their doctrine where the Russians are miscalculating, and in fact could be very dangerous and highly escalatory, despite their belief in the opposite.

Mr. ADERHOLT. Mr. Rademaker?

Mr. RADEMAKER. I would say that my concern is not just the fact that they're modernizing, because I think they have reasons that they can point to for wanting to do that. And they would argue it's essentially defensive in nature. But I think the reality is that they're not only modernizing, but they're now using their modernized military forces very actively. We see that in Ukraine. We see it in Syria. And I think it's that combination of not just modernization, but the willingness to deploy their forces and use force to try and effect outcomes on their periphery, but, as in the case of Syria, beyond their periphery.

Mr. ADERHOLT. Thank you.

Mr. WICKER. Thank you, Congressman Aderholt.

Senator Gardner.

HON. CORY GARDNER, COMMISSIONER, COMMISSION ON SECURITY AND COOPERATION IN EUROPE

Mr. GARDNER. Thank you, Senator Wicker.

And thank you to the witnesses for your time and testimony today.

I had the opportunity a couple of weeks ago to visit some of our soldiers out at Fort Carson and Colorado Springs, Colorado. It's the home of the 4th Infantry Division, the 10th Special Forces Group, and, of course, a lot of involvement in Atlantic Resolve and throughout Europe, various deployments over the past several years. In conversations I had with them, and obviously with our personnel at NATO, talked a lot about our muscle memory in Europe, and the fact that the United States over the past several decades, after the end of the Cold War, that we lost a lot of muscle memory when it comes to our activities, our presence, and our execution in Europe.

So, as it relates to Russia, what do you think is the most alarming loss of muscle memory in Europe? Is it on the intelligence side? Is it how to move quickly through Europe, if necessary? Does it go back to some of the RAND research that talks about the amount of time Russia, if they decided to go into Eastern Europe, could move and the speed with which they could accomplish that movement? Could you talk a little bit about muscle memory, those concerns?

Dr. CARPENTER. Senator, I would say that probably the number one concern is the inability of moving troops quickly through the European theater to the locus of a conflict. And so U.S. Army Europe has been focused on trying to build a "Schengen Zone for the military" to be able to get troops and supplies quickly to either the Baltic theater or the Black Sea theater in the event of a crisis there. But we're way behind the curve. And it takes a long time for the U.S. to be able to reinforce troops that are positioned on the front lines.

That, and I would say the other thing is simply the absence of force posture. So I think we're rectifying that problem right now with the deployment of an additional brigade combat team on a rotational basis. I would support deploying on a permanent basis an additional brigade combat team, armored above and beyond that. I think having armor, especially on the eastern flank of the alliance in the Baltic states, would be significant. It would be a large deterrent for Russia. And especially if it is manned by Americans, as opposed to the multinational brigades, which are a step in the right direction because they provide allied skin in the game. But there is nothing that substitutes for American presence on the eastern flank.

Mr. GARDNER. Anyone else care to comment?

Mr. RADEMAKER. I would volunteer the observation that, yes, there are important issues of American—what did you call it—muscle memory loss. But I think far more important than that has been muscle memory loss on the part of our allies. And I'm not talking about in the last year or two. I'm talking over the span of the last two decades, where I think a lot of our allies sort of got beyond the whole notion of NATO as an important defensive alliance, because they didn't really perceive a realistic Russian threat.

They didn't understand why they continued to need this alliance. And you saw reflected in their defense spending and their force structures that, you know, there really wasn't any expectation on their part that they were preparing or needed to be prepared for a situation where their security was actually threatened by Russia or some other external force.

The Russian actions in Ukraine, one collateral consequence of that has been that it has reminded some of our allies of the fact that contrary to their hope at the end of the Cold War, they do continue to live in an environment where there are security threats. And the NATO alliance and their own military investments continue to serve an important function for them. President Trump does seem to have elevated the importance of the issue of defense spending on the part of our allies. And I think we see some of them are now trying to get to the 2 percent threshold—the self-imposed threshold of NATO. So that would be a positive development, to see our allies start to regain some of the muscle memory.

Mr. GARDNER. Ambassador, did you want to add to that?

Amb. PIFER. I would agree that I think President Trump has brought allies to think more seriously about their defense contributions. It's also, I think, important for our European allies, though, to think about how they spend their money wisely, because if you do do a dollar-to-dollar comparison between American military spending and European military spending, we get much more in terms of deployable force than the Europeans do. And they have to be smarter about how they spend their money.

Mr. GARDNER. Part of that—the muscle memory was a conversation about the shift of our intelligence assets that went to the Middle East after the Cold War. And that that intelligence has never been necessarily rebuilt in Europe. Could you talk a little bit about our intelligence efforts with our allies in Europe, and how that stands today? What needs to be done?

Dr. CARPENTER. Senator, I think our intelligence in terms of—I don't want to go too far into this subject—but I think in terms of liaison relationships and human intelligence is pretty solid in Europe. Where I think we are less solid is in terms of ISR, for example, which is a high-demand, low-density platform that is being— all of those platforms are being sucked into the Middle East, where they're being used on a 24/7 basis. And so we have less coverage from an ISR, SIGINT-type perspective in Europe. But that is simply a product of not having enough of these systems to be able to satisfy the demand that is there, both in the European theater, in the Middle Eastern theater, and now, as well, in East Asia.

Mr. GARDNER. And I understand—we may be under a time limit—so I want to just have one quick question. Should we be entering into some kind of an intelligence agreement with Ukraine? Would that be a useful tool, more than we have today?

Amb. PIFER. Actually, we do have an agreement going to the 1990s. There is already——

Mr. GARDNER. On some of the cyber sharing issues, a little bit further.

Amb. PIFER. ——an exchange of classified military information. That is in place. And I think we now have an American unit in Yavoriv, in western Ukraine, training the Ukrainian military and the national guard. And my guess is we're actually learning quite a bit too, because some of the guys that we're training have actually been in Donbas. They've experienced the new Russian tactics. So this is actually a two-way exchange.

Mr. WICKER. Thank you, Senator Gardner.

Senator Rubio.

HON. MARCO RUBIO, COMMISSIONER, COMMISSION ON SECURITY AND COOPERATION IN EUROPE

Mr. RUBIO. Thank you, Mr. Chairman.

Thank you all for being in this meeting. I know I came in late. I may have missed some of your conversation about escalate in order to deescalate, the use of tactical nuclear weapons on the battlefield to kind of raise the specter of that.

Just to put it in perspective, the Russian economy is the size of the state of California, maybe even smaller. It's equivalent to Spain or Italy. So their ability to sustain the sort of broad defense posture the way the United States does across multiple potential theaters, it is limited. Nonetheless, they have shown the capability of spending more on that than wise policymakers would, because it's what gives them influence. Certainly, the nuclear stockpile's a different situation. It raises their influence above what their GDP would justify.

All that said, the one area that I don't know if it's been discussed, and falls with what I think is an emerging threat if not an already existent one, is the use of asymmetrical means on behalf of the Russians in any conflict. And we saw evidence of that both in Crimea and in Ukraine, also in Georgia in 2008, and the sort of electronic warfare that targets critical infrastructure, command and control—obviously there's an element of disinformation and propaganda that becomes associated with that as well. But this is an asymmetrical means of either escalating to de-escalate and/or denying your potential adversary some of their more advanced capabilities. And it is one that is quite cost effective, dollar for dollar.

So I don't know if that's been talked about enough, but perhaps—and then if you are prepared to talk a little bit more in depth about some of the means and measures used on behalf of the Russians in their intervention in Crimea and Ukraine and before that in Georgia in terms of the use of electronic warfare to target critical infrastructure—both civilian and military—and, of course, command and control and the like, because I think that ultimately will pose a threat first from Russia, but from other adversaries around the world as well as the years go on.

Dr. CARPENTER. Thank you, Senator. I would completely agree with you. I think you see an evolution in terms of Russian doctrine from a largely conventional war in Georgia to an unconventional war, where they used special forces, little green men, in Ukraine, to a military intelligence organized coup d'état in Montenegro, that was luckily foiled, to political subversion campaigns across the United States and Western Europe.

They are both expanding the geographic scope of their gray zone operations, but they are also increasingly moving from conventional military force to more covert, subversion measures. And I think it's because it's cheaper, it's easier, and it's likely more effective. But, in both Ukraine and Georgia, while they were able to stall Euro-Atlantic integration, the populations have become rather pro-Western—have stayed pro-Western or become even more so, and have developed some hostility towards Moscow.

Mr. RUBIO. And obviously, I know it's been extensively discussed and I think it's very relevant and a big threat. I'm going beyond just that. I'm talking about the ability to shut down power grids, the ability to shut down command and control. The ability to shut down or attack the banking sector. The sorts of critical infrastructure attack that we saw some evidence of that in the Ukraine-Crimea situation. Saw some of that even before that in the Georgia 2007–2008 timeframe. That's one that's not getting a lot of attention, but I think poses a real threat. And I have no doubt we would see deployed in any sort of Eastern European conflict or potential conflict, especially nations that perhaps have not invested in hardening against that sort of intrusion.

Dr. CARPENTER. Well, that is primarily, Senator, a cyber threat more so than an electronic warfare threat. But it has been deployed, as you say, in Georgia and Ukraine. And we know the Russians have penetrated a lot of U.S. Government networks, the networks of our allies as well. So their ability potentially to be able to shut down critical infrastructure is enormous. I mean, they have shut down electric power plants in Ukraine. They have penetrated networks in other allied countries, including Ministry of Defense networks in a lot of our allies. And so this is something that we need to work on, both here domestically but also in terms of building up the cyber defenses of our allies. It's critically important. This is potentially one of the most lethal threats that we face, even if it is non-kinetic.

Mr. RUBIO. And just in closing I would say that the proper terminology is probably cyber. The reason why I always kind of describe it a little differently is because when people think of cyber in the public they're thinking, oh, they're going to hack my emails. This is way more than hacking emails. We're talking about shutting down potentially a power grid and the like. And in a conflict, everyone could imagine how debilitating that would be to any nation-state, particularly some of these Eastern European NATO allies that would probably be on the front lines of any such effort.

Mr. WICKER. A health care system, for example, Senator Rubio.

Mr. RUBIO. [the lights in the room dimmed briefly] They just did it right now. [Laughter.] There you go. There you go. [Laughter.]

Mr. WICKER. You spoke it and it happened. [Laughter.]

Senator Cardin.

HON. BENJAMIN L. CARDIN, RANKING MEMBER, COMMISSION ON SECURITY AND COOPERATION IN EUROPE

Mr. CARDIN. Well, thank you, Mr. Chairman. I apologize for being late. I had a couple other committees that I had to participate in.

But I just really want to underscore the importance of this hearing and thank our witnesses. It's very interesting. I've been dealing with Russian policy for a long time—from the former Soviet Union. Russia has violated every one of the Helsinki Final Act's 10 guiding principles—every single one. And I've sat across from Russian parliamentarians where they complained that we tried to interfere with their internal operations, even though the Helsinki Final Act gives us the responsibility to raise violations. And we're not interfering with their country.

But then Russia directly attacks other member states, as they did with Ukraine, the most recent. It wasn't the first country that they violated. They were involved in Moldova. They were involved in Georgia. Ten thousand people lost their lives as a result of the military incursions in Ukraine. So it has deadly consequences. And many, many thousands have been displaced. I mention that because Russia's dangerous. And the United States policies need to recognize that danger.

So I guess my question is that Russia seems to go in wherever there are voids. They see an opportunity where we don't have a NATO member in Europe, where there's some chaos. They come in and try to stir it up, and then bring their military presence in to cause instability, trying to weaken the European Union, trying to weaken the transatlantic partnership. So where's their next move in Europe? Where do you see the vulnerabilities that could lead to Russia's military operations in an effort to stir up problems?

There's a lot of countries in Europe that have large Russian-speaking populations. Where would you want us to focus on concerns where other countries could become prey to Russian aggression? We know they don't always use their direct soldiers. They send in resources. They use a local population that they have influence over. Where do we think the next attack is likely to occur?

Amb. PIFER. Senator, I would continue to worry about the Baltic states. I don't think Russian military action against the Baltics is likely. But it's not a zero probability. And I think if we were having this hearing five or six years ago, we would have said it was a zero probability. So I'd worry about that. But it does get to your point that we need to make clear to the Kremlin that there are red lines. I hope that when the President is in Brussels at the NATO summit next week that there's a very clear American commitment to Article 5, because we don't want the Russians to miscalculate and believe falsely that the United States would not respond to military action against an ally.

Likewise, I think on questions like the Russians' loose talk about nuclear weapons and escalate to de-escalate, we should begin to devalue that notion in the mind of the Russians right now by basically saying: Look, a nuclear weapon is a nuclear weapon. If you use one, even if it's a small one, you still have crossed a threshold that has not been crossed in 70 years, and you should anticipate that the consequences would be unpredictable and potentially catastrophic. And in the case of Ukraine, we should make very clear that a major Russian offensive will lead to major consequences. Not sending the American military, but new economic sanctions and a certain American military support.

We need to begin to shape Russian thinking, that they have to understand that there are certain places that the West will not tolerate Russian overreach and will push back on. And hopefully, as we shape that thinking, maybe Moscow comes around to a more accommodating view on some of these questions. Because red lines

are going to be important if we want to make our dialogue ultimately be more successful.

Mr. CARDIN. Well, NATO has red lines. I would think that that
is pretty clear. If we don't enforce the red lines in NATO, I think
we have serious challenges. But you raise a very valid point. We've
been, in the first months of this Congress, playing defense to try
to maintain our sanctions against Russia, both internally as well
as in Europe. And we have been able to maintain our sanctions.
But Russia's activities have gotten worse. They're much more aggressive. The cyber activities that we talked about—much more aggressive. So without U.S. leadership on saying there's a consequence to that, it's very, very unlikely that you'll see Europe do
much without the United States taking the lead.

So we don't see any leadership from the Trump Administration
in using stronger sanctions against Russia. The congressional
branch of government needs to show leadership here. And we have
a bipartisan bill that has strong support. Senator McCain is my co-
sponsor, and Senator Shaheen is one of the great leaders on that
bill. And we've had the support of Senator Graham and Senator
Rubio, and Senator Wicker has been an outspoken supporter of
taking a strong stance against Russia. We need to take some action
here in Congress. Do you agree with that?

Amb. PIFER. Yes, sir. One of the things I worry about is that if
the West response in the case of Ukraine is not sufficiently strong,
does the Kremlin conclude that the tactics that they've employed
against Ukraine over the last few years can be managed at accept-
able cost? In which case, they might be tempted to use them elsewhere. Likewise, I think that there should be a stronger American
reaction to the Russian interference in our election. Right now, my
guess is at the Kremlin they're thinking, you know, this doesn't
have many costs and it's pretty tempting to try it again, as we've
seen in France and as I believe we're going to see in the next three
or four months in Germany.

Mr. CARDIN. Thank you.

Mr. WICKER. Glad to hear that there's bipartisan support for
stronger action on sanctions. And I think, Senator Cardin, before
you came in there was testimony to the effect that the Magnitsky
list should be expanded by the State Department. And I know you
and I support that also.

We're going to take a second round. Congressman Smith will go
next and then I'll follow him.

Mr. SMITH. Thank you very much, Mr. Chairman.

And thank you for your testimonies.

Both my older brothers were military pilots. One of my brothers,
Tom, flew A-7s off the USS Enterprise. As in control as fighter pilots are, and we had a conversation about this last week, my broth-
er expressed to me his deep concern that the probability of an inci-
dent, a collision, increases exponentially with the number and
proximity of these very provocative acts, these near-misses that are
occurring with increasing frequency. I wonder if any of you might
want to speak to what's behind this reckless behavior. Again, a
pilot might think that he can, you know, break off. But it's going
to happen, I think. There are just too many of them, that something is going to happen. What's behind this reckless behavior?

And are the two-way communications between ourselves and the Russians—NATO and the Russians sufficiently adequate to mitigate any kind of escalation, both immediate in proximity to what's happening, and maybe even a further escalation into war by miscalculation?

Dr. CARPENTER. Congressman, I believe that a lot of these aggressive intercepts are part of a deliberate strategy. You just have to contrast how Russia behaves in the Baltic or the Black Sea with how they behave in Syria, where we have a deconfliction channel and where our pilots are in very close proximity in a very congested air space, and manage to avoid these sorts of incidents. I personally don't believe that any sort of new communication channels or agreements on transponders, as has been proposed, will have any effect on Russian behavior, because the desire on the part of the Kremlin is to intimidate, to send a message, to keep the United States, but also our NATO allies, out of their backyard.

And so if they see any diminution of our ops tempo, of our operations, in these regions, they will conclude that this is a successful strategy and will continue with it. And so my view is that we need to continue with our ops tempo exactly as it is. But this is certainly dangerous behavior, endangering the lives of both American and Russian air crews.

Amb. PIFER. I agree with Mike that I think this is actually a part of deliberate Russian policy to raise this risk of accident and miscalculation. But I don't think there's anything that the United States or NATO lose by trying to set up channels. So, for example, in 1989 we had the Dangerous Military Activities Agreement that regulated U.S. and Soviet forces along the inter-German border. I wonder if a resurrection of something like that might make sense now in the Baltic and the Polish region, where you do have NATO forces on a border directly facing Russian forces.

And that Dangerous Military Activities Agreement had things like, for example, agreed radio channels where, if you saw the guy on the other side of the border doing something that you didn't understand, you had a channel. Call and say: What are you doing? Things like that. I'm not sure the Russians would accept that, but I see no harm and potential value to NATO in trying to engage Russia on those sorts of channels, because the sides presumably should not have an interest in war breaking out, just because somebody makes a mistake or misunderstands what a young Russian pilot is doing.

Mr. SMITH. Thank you, Mr. Chairman.

Mr. WICKER. Thank you.

Gentlemen, let's talk about Russia's destabilizing transfers to neighboring and regional countries of threatening weapons systems. Just this past year, Russia delivered the S-300 missile system to OSCE member state Belarus, with a range of upwards of 250 kilometers. Russia has also positioned the Iskander-M missile system to its base in Kaliningrad, which has the capability of carrying a nuclear payload within 500-kilometer radius. As a matter of fact, the Lithuanian foreign minister said in October of last year that with some modifications this could go to 700 kilometers, which would then include Berlin. Also, Russia has transferred the Iskander-E missile system to OSCE member state Armenia. How troubling is this? And would you three gentlemen have comments on these destabilizing arms transfers and how they are stoking tensions throughout Europe and Eurasia?

Mr. Rademaker.

Mr. RADEMAKER. Thank you, Mr. Chairman. There's a long history to destabilizing Russian transfers to countries of concern. I recall during the 1990s, there was great concern about missile technology transfers by Russia to Iran. And, in fact, Congress enacted legislation—the Iran Nonproliferation Act—directed at precisely that issue—seeking to impose sanctions on Russian entities that were involved in making such transfers. That law, aimed at what were violations by Russia of its obligations under various supplier regimes for limiting exports of sensitive technology and systems. And, you know, these regimes exist under the Nuclear Nonproliferation Treaty. That one's called the nuclear suppliers group. They exist under the chemical weapons and biological convention. That's called the Australia Group. The missile technology control regime exists to limit missile technology transfers.

Some of the transfers you alluded to violate these regimes. The S-300, that's not a ballistic missile so the transfer of that is not limited by the missile technology control regime, but it's nonetheless a destabilizing transfer. And you didn't mention the transfer of S-300s to Iran, but that's another step that the Russians have taken, over strong U.S. objections. The Iskander missile, which you referred to, that is a ballistic missile.

My understanding is there are two versions of the Iskander. There's the Iskander-M, which is a roughly 500-kilometer range. Transfers of that are limited by the missile technology control regime. Russia is presumptively not to transfer that technology to anybody. Then there's the Iskander-E, which is—E I think stands for export. It's supposed to be the export-controlled version, which has a range less than 300 kilometers. So it could be transferred consistent with the missile technology control regime.

Obviously when they deploy it in their own territory, in Kaliningrad, that's not a transfer to anybody. But if they transfer it to a country like Armenia, then the key question is which version did they transfer? Was it the E or the M? If it was the E, then it was consistent with the missile technology control regime. If it was the M, it would be inconsistent. I've actually seen conflicting press accounts of which version was transferred to Armenia.

Mr. WICKER. Ambassador.

Amb. PIFER. Mr. Chairman, I actually tend to be pessimistic about our ability to stop some of these things. I mean, the Russians will argue, for example, on the S-300 sale to Belarus, they're saying Belarus is one of the few countries in the world that would say is an ally of Russia. And they would say that providing that air defense system to Belarus is the same as, for example, the United States selling the Patriot Air Defense system to Poland.

On Iskander to Kaliningrad, from what I've seen, the Iskander, they're in the 4- to 500-kilometer range, which is not covered by the INF Treaty, the ballistic missile. It seems to be that the Russians are now, basically as they phase out the SS-21, which was their previous short range surface-to-surface missile, those units are now receiving the Iskander. From what I've seen, the Iskander has been deployed temporarily with exercises in Kaliningrad, but the Russians previously had SS-21 permanently based there. And it's my expectation that at some point you'll see the Iskander in Kaliningrad. So we'll have to think about, on the NATO side, what are the sorts of defenses that you would want to be able to deal with that system. But I don't think we're going to be able to persuade the Russians not to go forward with it.

Mr. WICKER. Thank you.

Senator Shaheen.

Mrs. SHAHEEN. Thank you, Mr. Chairman.

I want to follow up on Senator Cardin's question about where do we expect the Russians may agitate next in Europe, because I'm very concerned about reports that are coming out of the Balkans, particularly in Bosnia and Serbia and Kosovo, where it seems they're agitating to try and prevent further calming of the conflict between Serbia and Kosovo, and also where they're ginning up the Republika Srpska, since we mentioned that, to continue to try to agitate to leave Bosnia and really play on some of the tensions that exist in the region. So I wonder if you all can comment on that, and what you're hearing, and also what should we be doing as we think about the challenges that the Balkans are facing to try and support their continued move towards democracy and integration in the EU and the West.

Dr. CARPENTER. Well, thank you for that question, Senator. I was going to reply to Senator Cardin's question with precisely this answer: That the Western Balkans is in the crosshairs of Russian influence operations right now, particularly Republika Srpska, where they have been encouraging President Dodik to pursue his secessionist agenda. And we could see, in fact, within the course of a year, that a referendum will be declared on the succession of Republika Srpska from Bosnia and Herzegovina. They have also been intervening in Macedonia, supporting Mr. Gruevski and accusing the United States of trying to subvert the previous government and of meddling. But this is now being superimposed—this political tension between the former ruling party, VMRO, and the opposition, SDSM, with an ethic overlay between ethnic Albanians who are members of the coalition and ethnic Macedonians.

And so the potential for this spinning out of control and creating a full-fledged ethnic conflict in the Western Balkans is, in my view, very high. And I mentioned the plot for a coup d'état in Montenegro in October—across the whole region Russia is meddling and trying to subvert some of the governments and sow chaos and instability. And so I think for us, we just simply need to get more engaged in the Balkans. We need to support the Belgrade-Pristina Dialogue. We need to support those in Bosnia and Herzegovina that want to activate MAP and move forward with their NATO integration process. I'm not saying membership, just MAP, which is has been held up for very artificial reasons over the issue of registration of defense properties.

But when I was at the A5 Defense Ministerial in December of last year, I heard from absolutely everybody across the board—including quietly from the Serbian delegation—that Russia was playing an outsized role in every country in the region.

Mr. WICKER. Tell us about what the Serbian leadership's position would be with regard to this proposed possible referendum in Republika Srpska.

Dr. CARPENTER. Very much opposed. But of course, the previous Serbian prime minister, Aleksander Vucic, is now the president of Serbia. And so when we have a new prime minister, which is where most of the executive authority in Serbia is vested, we will see whether they will pursue that policy of trying to push back Dodik's more aggressive moves in Republika Srpska and Banja Luka, or whether they will, in fact, stand by or potentially support them more. In fact, the decision on who will become the next prime minister will be a bit of litmus test as far as whether Serbia is hedging more towards Moscow or more towards Brussels.

Mrs. SHAHEEN. Any other comments anybody wants to make on that issue?

Mr. RADEMAKER. Senator, I noted in the conclusion of my testimony that Russia's approach to the region really is based on a zero-sum view of security, that they think keeping their neighbors weak and vulnerable keeps them stronger. And I think you see that in looking over the last 10 or 15 years in their policies towards some of their neighbors. What is very interesting is, though, that they do—hopefully for the right reasons—they do seem to be respecting the lines that NATO draws. They have focused their efforts on countries that are not NATO members. And of course, as members of NATO, we have no obligation to defend non-NATO members. I think the Georgians discovered that, to their chagrin, in 2008. But it was true. Ukraine has discovered it more recently.

The Western Balkans is an area that, by and large, lies outside of NATO. And therefore, I think for Russia, it presents an opportunity. And it is something that I think we need to be deeply concerned about. I also worry—as Ambassador Pifer noted in responding to Senator Cardin's question—if the Russians ever decide to press or look beyond the NATO borders, I think the area most at risk would be the Baltic states, which, of course, were a part of the Soviet Union and therefore arguably part of the Russian near-abroad, where they've asserted publicly they think they're entitled to have a special security role.

So we need to be alert to use by Russia of some of these new tools that Senator Rubio referred to, if they're brought to bear in the Baltic states. Whether we're prepared as an alliance to respond to that, I'm concerned that we're not. So the ultimate solution is a change in the Russian mindset, where they stop approaching the world with this zero-sum mentality to security issues. But until we get to that point, I think we need to worry especially about the countries in Europe that are not in NATO. But also some of the countries in NATO which border Russia; I think we need to be concerned about them as well.

Mrs. SHAHEEN. And that speaks to Ambassador Pifer's comment about being very clear that we are committed to maintaining Article 5 for all of our NATO allies.

Amb. PIFER. And if I could just briefly add on the Balkans, I am mindful of that when you look at the U.S. global focus, I worry that the Balkans may not get sufficient U.S. attention.

Mrs. SHAHEEN. Me too.

Amb. PIFER. The Balkans, to my mind——

Mr. WICKER. Me too.

Mrs. SHAHEEN. Yes.

Amb. PIFER. The Balkans, to my mind, actually would be a place where I'd like to see Europe lead, where the European Union has traction. This ought to be a focus. And so if we could somehow encourage Europe to take that role, that would be a good thing.

I'm also mindful—I served at the American embassy in London in the early 1990s, and we watched Europe take the lead the first time when Yugoslavia came apart, and it didn't work out well, and ultimately the United States did have to get involved. But at some point we need to figure out, is there a way where Europe can begin to take on some of these responsibilities, because we're going to have to be thinking about other issues that are outside of Europe.

Mr. WICKER. You know, we've drawn such bright lines and made such explicit statements with regard to the Baltic countries. I do sort of fear that we haven't been as explicit with regard to the former Yugoslavia, and so I share some of your concerns there. Help us understand this attempted coup in October and whether we should be worried about similar efforts.

Dr. CARPENTER. Absolutely, Mr. Chairman. I think this could be the wave of the future in terms of how Russia tries to destabilize countries in the region.

Mr. WICKER. So tell our audience in a nutshell what happened there.

Dr. CARPENTER. In a nutshell, a small number of Russian military intelligence agents organized and planned a coup d'état on Election Day in October in Montenegro. They hired approximately 20 local mercenaries from Serbia and from Montenegro, members of organized crime groups and radical nationalist circles. They were to dress in Montenegrin police uniforms and fire on protesters outside of parliament on the day of the election in order to incite chaos and assassinate the prime minister. Now, in order to ensure that there would be protesters who turned out on Election Day, Russia also used covert means to fund opposition political parties and NGOs through cutouts in Montenegro. And they also perpetrated cyberattacks on Election Day. They both shut down government networks so that the authorities in Podgorica would not be able to communicate the election results to their citizenry, but they also hijacked social media platforms like Viber and WhatsApp to spread fake news and disinformation claiming that the vote count had been rigged and tampered with. This was an attempt to get protesters to come out.

Now, the coup plot was foiled in advance thanks to good intelligence and a tipoff.

Mr. WICKER. How early?

Dr. CARPENTER. But the cyberattacks took place.

Mr. WICKER. How early was it foiled?

Dr. CARPENTER. I would have to address that in a closed session.

Mr. WICKER. Oh my gosh. OK. But this could certainly occur again, particularly in a relatively small and vulnerable republic.

Dr. CARPENTER. Absolutely. I couldn't agree more. And I think the Western Balkans, as I said, are in the crosshairs for this type of action.

Mr. WICKER. Yes, please. Mr. Rademaker.

Mr. RADEMAKER. I just wanted to add the detail that all of this took place in a context where Montenegro was in the process of acceding to NATO. And so success of the coup there might have—depending on whatever government came to power, might have ended their NATO accession process.

Mr. WICKER. Is there any question that Mr. Putin was involved in this?

Dr. CARPENTER. No question in my mind.

Mr. WICKER. Mr. Rubio mentioned the economy of Russia being about the size of Spain. We are trying to insist on 2 percent of GDP for our NATO allies. What percent of GDP does Russia spend? And are they going to have a problem sustaining this military modernization and buildup?

Amb. PIFER. The Russian economy, I think, is projected to grow at about 1.2 percent this year. And I don't know—I think it was about—what, 5 percent that they hit at one point, but the number's actually coming down now, and I think it's reflecting the fact that the Russians understand that there are budgetary limitations. In 2015, they began reducing the budgets for things like health and education, but this year and next year they're projecting significant decreases in military spending. Now, part of that may also reflect the fact that a lot of their modernization has already been funded, but they are beginning to run up against some budget realities.

Dr. CARPENTER. Although, if I could, I would just say I don't think we can be too sanguine that they will not be able to continue the tempo that they have in Syria or Ukraine because their reserves remain just under $400 billion. So they have a significant amount of reserves that they've built up through the 2000s, when oil prices were very high, that they can still draw on to be able to perpetuate these sorts of actions in Ukraine and elsewhere.

Mr. WICKER. And, finally, in the area of public diplomacy, Russia eats our lunch. Does anyone agree with that or disagree with that and want to comment about it? And how can we do a better job without becoming a propaganda organ of getting public information to people in that region of the world? Do they eat our lunch? Am I wrong?

Dr. CARPENTER. No, Chairman, I think they do. Not in the United States, but I think their ability to perpetrate information warfare in places like Moldova or Georgia especially, where a lot of attitudes have shifted over the last couple years in both of those countries, but also in the Baltic states, is very robust.

And so I think one of the means of pushing back has to be to inoculate the populations to what Russia is doing. Actually, you find that the Baltic states are quite good at this. There has been an education campaign by the governments in the Baltic states. The population knows that false stories come out of Russian media, and the mainstream media are also very quick to debunk Russian stories.

So, for example, when the multinational battalions were deployed to the Baltic states and Russian media started to propagate fake stories about alleged rapes that had taken place by some of the soldiers who are on these territories, immediately the Baltic media were able to clarify that this was false, disinformation, and correct the record. And so they have a lot of experience with this. And I think, you know, some of the Western European countries and here in the United States——

Mr. WICKER. And yet, the Baltic media is independent of the government.

Dr. CARPENTER. It is. The governments of some of the Baltic states, particularly Estonia, also fund Russian-language media, television—broadcast television which is able to get the message out to the Estonian ethnic Russian, Russian-speaking population.

Amb. PIFER. I would add that the Russians devote a lot of resources to this. I recall about two years ago, when I was in Prague, and I turned on the television. I could not find CNN, but I could find RT in English, RT high-def in English, and RT in Spanish.

Mr. WICKER. Shouldn't we be investing more resources?

Amb. PIFER. I think we should be investing resources, but I would focus on what I believe is the vulnerability of both RT and Sputnik, is that there's a lot of bad information they put out, and the focus should be on discrediting those channels. And then, basically, we want a situation where a target audience in Europe, when they hear something, they say, that's just RT, we know they lie. And that's an area where perhaps we could do better in terms of fast reaction to discredit the stories immediately when they come out. If we discredit a story five days later, it doesn't really help. But if we can come out immediately and say this is false, here's the evidence, I think we can take down those channels, and reduce their credibility and their potential impact.

Mr. WICKER. Mr. Rademaker.

Mr. RADEMAKER. Mr. Chairman, I would just add the observation that in the area of information warfare there's sort of the overt and then there's the covert. And I think in the overt area, which is what we've been talking about here, you know, Russia does a reasonably good job. Although I have to say I occasionally watch RT, and to me it's kind of laughable. I mean, it is sort of thinly-veiled propaganda and I don't take it seriously. I don't know whether average citizens find it more persuasive, but you know, I——

Mrs. SHAHEEN. They do.

Mr. WICKER. I'm afraid they do.

Mr. RADEMAKER. Yes. But I worry actually less about that than I do the covert side because during the Cold War I believe both sides were engaged in covert efforts to generate information in support of their political objectives. I think Russia remains in that business, especially in Europe. I don't think the United States is very much in that business anymore.

And so, it turns out, there's a very active environmental movement against fracking in Europe and against the construction of the southern energy corridor, and it's pretty clear the money for this environmental movement, a lot of it's coming from Moscow. And what's Russia's concern? Well, you know, it would be nice for Europe to remain dependent on Gazprom and not have alternate sources of energy, either domestic through fracking in countries like Poland or gas that comes from the Caucasus. So that's just one example.

And I think support to political parties that have agendas that are amenable to Russia is another area. Senator Whitehouse referred to that in his question. I think this is an area where Russia has pretty much a free hand and no one is pushing back on them. And I don't think there's even really much effort to call them out on it and expose what the Russians are doing in that area.

Mr. WICKER. Do we need to revamp the Broadcasting Board of Governors in this country, Dr. Carpenter?

Dr. CARPENTER. I would say—well, the BBG has got some good programs. It's recently launched a program called "Current Time," which is a digital Russian-language platform that reaches Russian-speaking audiences on Russia's periphery and inside—and it's digital, so it can be picked up on the internet in Russia as well. Unfortunately, it doesn't compete with the more glossy Russian broadcast TV channels that offer attractive entertainment programming as well.

I would support putting more resources into this sort of effort, but I don't think it's going to be the be-all and end-all of countering Russian disinformation. I think we've got to be more active on the offense as well. I think we need to be talking more about corrupt patterns within Russia. Some of the information, for example, that has been brought to light by Alexei Navalny's organization, that has wide currency in Russia. And if we were able to not just play Whac-a-Mole with Russian disinformation and lies, but also spread some of this information, I think that would be highly effective in terms of pushing back.

Mr. RADEMAKER. Mr. Chairman, if I could just add, particularly if there is additional information available to the U.S. intelligence community that could be declassified on Russian corruption, I think that would actually be a proper response to what the Russians did to our election, and basically signal the Kremlin: If you want to play this game, we may not be able to play it in the same way, but I'm sure that the Kremlin would not like to see more information about the corruption and the billions of dollars held by people that are close to Vladimir Putin.

Mr. WICKER. Thank you, gentlemen, and thank you to our panel and the members of the Commission who participated. And also, thank you to our audience today. This hearing is now adjourned.

[Whereupon, at 11:21 a.m., the hearing ended.]

APPENDICES

PREPARED STATEMENTS

PREPARED STATEMENT OF HON. ROGER F. WICKER, CO-CHAIRMAN, COMMISSION ON SECURITY AND COOPERATION IN EUROPE

The Commission will come to order, and good morning to everybody. Welcome to today's hearing on the "Growing Russian Military Threat in Europe."

This is the Commission's second hearing of this Congress. Our first hearing, on April 26, rightly focused on human rights abuses within Russia. Today's hearing will examine Russian actions beyond its borders—specifically Moscow's use of military force to further its ambitions.

The mandate of the Helsinki Commission requires us to "monitor the acts of the signatories which reflect compliance with or violation of the articles of the Final Act of the Conference on Security and Cooperation in Europe," also known as the Helsinki Final Act.

Even a casual observer of international affairs would recognize that Russian military aggression has posed a tremendous threat to the European security order in recent years. The Russian leadership has chosen an antagonistic stance, both regionally and globally, as it seeks to reassert its influence from a bygone era.

The actions taken by the Russian leadership under this aggressive posture have without any doubt violated commitments enshrined in the Helsinki Final Act and other agreements. To name three key examples:

1. Russia has breached its commitment to refrain from the threat or use of force against other states;

2. Russia has breached its commitment to refrain from violating their sovereignty, territorial integrity or political independence; and

3. Russia has breached its commitment to respect other states' right to choose their own security alliances.

Many of Russia's neighbors have faced Russian military aggression in recent years. Ukraine and Georgia have both seen important parts of their territories forcibly occupied, including the illegal attempted annexation of Crimea in 2014. Russian forces continue to be present in Ukraine, Georgia, and Moldova, against the wishes of the governments of those countries.

In addition to its direct aggression toward its neighbors, Moscow has also made it a priority to undermine the effective functioning of several conventional arms control agreements and measures for confidence and security building. These measures, to which Russia is a party, include:

1. The Treaty on Conventional Armed Forces in Europe, which limits heavy ground and air weapons in Europe and provides information on current arms holdings, including their location;

2. The Open Skies Treaty, which provides for mutual unarmed aerial reconnaissance of member states; and

3. The Vienna Document on Confidence- and Security-Building Measures, which provides for information exchanges, on-site inspections, and notifications of the military activities, arms, and force levels of OSCE participating States.

These agreements—along with others, such as the INF Treaty, which Russia is also violating—together form an interlocking web of commitments that have proved fundamental to the stability of the post-Cold War European security architecture. They were designed to enhance military transparency and predictability, thereby increasing confidence among the OSCE participating States.

Unfortunately, the actions of the Russian leadership in recent years have demonstrated that Russia sees little value in the transparency and predictability that have kept the peace in Europe.

I would like to make one more point. I want to reiterate my dismay regarding the tragic death of American paramedic Joseph Stone on April 23. Mr. Stone was killed while serving his country as a member of the OSCE Special Monitoring Mission in Ukraine when his vehicle struck an explosive—likely a landmine—in separatist-controlled territory, an event that also injured two other monitors.

This is the first time in the history of the OSCE that a mission member has been killed in the line of duty, and make no mistake, Mr. Stone's death was directly related to Russia's aggression towards its neighbors. Had Russia not invaded Ukraine in the first place—and had it lived up to the Minsk agreements, and ceased supporting, directing, funding, and fueling separatists in this region—there would have been no need for the monitoring mission to continue. Once again, I extend my condolences to Mr. Stone's family and friends.

I also want to take this opportunity to call for an end to the harassment faced by these brave monitors on a daily basis, and I urge all sides to provide the observers with unfettered access.

We have put a photograph of OSCE monitors in the room as a reminder of the continuing challenges faced by these brave monitors as they carry out their extremely important mission.

Our hearing today has three objectives. We will:

1. Examine Russia's undermining of European security, the OSCE, and its arms control agreements and commitments;

2. Assess whether it will be possible to move Russia back toward compliance with its commitments under the Helsinki Final Act and the associated OSCE agreements, and if so, how to get there; and

3. Finally, explore how we can maximize the value of these agreements and the OSCE as a whole going forward.

I am grateful to the members of our distinguished panel for their willingness to provide expert views on these topics, and I look forward to our discussion today.

PREPARED STATEMENT OF HON. CHRIS SMITH, CO-CHAIRMAN, COMMISSION ON SECURITY AND COOPERATION IN EUROPE

Good morning and thank you to Chairman Wicker for convening this important hearing to examine Russian military aggression in the OSCE region.

Russia today stands in violation of the central commitments of the Helsinki Final Act. These commitments include respect for the territorial integrity of States, fundamental freedoms, and the fulfillment in good faith of obligations under international law. In violating these commitments, Russia is threatening the foundations of European security and recklessly endangering the lives of millions.

One such victim of Russian aggression is Joseph Stone, the 36-year-old American medic who was killed by a landmine while on patrol in separatist-controlled eastern Ukraine with the OSCE's Special Monitoring Mission on April 23rd. If it weren't for Russia's unjustifiable aggression toward Ukraine's sovereignty there would be no need for such a monitoring mission. And yet, day after day, OSCE monitors put themselves in harm's way to try to reduce the tensions created by the reckless conduct of Russia and its proxies in eastern Ukraine. It is a conflict that has already claimed over ten thousand lives, and sadly is guaranteed to claim more.

Russian aggression is not a localized phenomenon—it threatens the entire region. Moscow has seized sovereign territory by force, threatened to use tactical nuclear weapons against other countries, harassed U.S. and Allied military assets, and abandoned key transparency measures and commitments. These actions are unacceptable.

In the face of such provocations, the United States must leave no doubt that we stand behind our Eastern European and Baltic Allies. There is no time to waste: we must ensure the confidence of our friends at this critical juncture.

One way to do this is to continue building a credible conventional deterrent to Russian aggression alongside our allies, in particular Poland and the Baltic States. I have consistently supported robust funding for the European Reassurance Initiative. With the support of this initiative, since 2014, NATO members have held over 1,000 military exercises in Europe. ERI has allowed the U.S. to participate more extensively in such exercises and increase its deployment of soldiers and military assets in allied countries. Furthermore, it has helped us to build the capacity of our partners and generally make our commitment to European security felt. These kinds of activities must be sustained and expanded to ensure that we are ready to counter any threat at any time.

This hearing will give us an opportunity to learn what more the U.S. can do on this front, both bilaterally and within NATO. In particular, I look forward to Dr. Carpenter's testimony about the extent of the challenge posed by Russian aggression in the OSCE region; Mr. Rademaker's thoughts about the implications of Russia's flouting of its arms control and transparency commitments; and Ambassador Pifer's perspective on developments in Ukraine and what they mean for the region. I will also be interested to hear from our witnesses about the role of the OSCE in all of this.

To all our witnesses, I thank you for your time today.

PREPARED STATEMENT OF HON. BENJAMIN L. CARDIN, RANKING MEMBER,
COMMISSION ON SECURITY AND COOPERATION IN EUROPE

Chairman Wicker, thank you for convening this hearing and for your leadership of the Helsinki Commission. This hearing could not be more timely.

I have said before that Russia is violating every single one of the Helsinki Final Act's ten Guiding Principles between states. Many of us have drawn attention to Russia's violation of principles on sovereign equality, on territorial integrity and on the inviolability of borders. If I may, Mr. Chairman, today I'd like to put a little bit of a spotlight on Principle VI—"non-intervention in internal affairs."

Russia has long sought to counter discussion of human rights by claiming that raising human rights concerns is "interference" or "intervention" in internal affairs. This, of course, is not true. In fact, the OSCE participating States explicitly agreed in 1991 that raising human rights issues is *not* interference in the internal affairs of other states.

What does "non-intervention in the internal affairs" of other countries mean then? Well, when the participating States adopted Principle VI in the 1975 Helsinki Final Act, they were rejecting the Brezhnev Doctrine and the Soviet invasions of Hungary and Czechoslovakia. Principle VI expressly prohibits "armed intervention or threat of such intervention against another participating State." That agreement was an important basis for building many of the subsequent agreements we were able to achieve in the OSCE, including many in the area of military security.

But under President Putin, Russia has systematically undermined all of the security arrangements that peacefully ended the Cold War. When Russia invaded Georgia in 2008 and Ukraine in 2014, they not only violated this principle of the Helsinki Accords, they turned back the clock to the days of the Brezhnev era. In the Helsinki Final Act, the participating States pledged to refrain from making each other's territory the object of military occupation in contravention of international law. Today, Russia is manifestly violating that commitment.

And the costs of Russia's aggression continue to mount. Some 10,000 people have been killed in Ukraine and hundreds of thousands displaced. 298 people were killed when Russian-backed separatists shot down the civilian flight MH17. A week ago, Joseph Stone, an American member of the OSCE Special Monitoring Mission in Ukraine was killed and two others, a Czech and a German national, were injured by a land mine in Russian-backed separatist controlled territory. I join you, Mr. Chairman, in expressing grief at this senseless loss of life and anger at those who are responsible.

Russia is the greatest threat to the security of Europe and the United States. Accordingly, I welcome this hearing's examination of the Russian military threat, particularly in the context of the OSCE framework for confidence- and security-building, and I look forward to working with you and other members of the Commission to protect the security of the United States and our allies. I regret that there continue to be so many positions that the administration has yet to fill at a time when our country faces such acute threats and hope that the administration will move quickly to fill key senior positions in the State Department and Department of Defense.

PREPARED STATEMENT OF HON. MICHAEL BURGESS, COMMISSIONER, COMMISSION ON SECURITY AND COOPERATION IN EUROPE

In 2014, Russia used military force to breach the borders of Ukraine and annex Crimea. Despite an official ceasefire, known as Minsk II, Russia's actions and non-implementation of the ceasefire have produced a frozen conflict that has killed at least 10,000 people. This aggression directly violates the guiding principles of the Helsinki Final Act, including sovereign equality for member states, refraining from the threat or use of force, ensuring the territorial integrity of states, and non-intervention in internal affairs. In addition, Russia has been engaging in overt and covert subversive action in the media and in cyberspace domestically and across international borders in order to further an aggressive agenda.

Russia has either violated or completely ignored provisions of the Treaty on Conventional Armed Forced in Europe, the Open Skies Treaty, the Vienna Document, and the Intermediate-Range Nuclear Forces Treaty. This posturing clearly indicates Russia's unwillingness to cooperate with its European neighbors to improve security. In fact, Russia views its security as directly proportional to the insecurity of its European neighbors.

Vladimir Putin wants NATO to fracture and international organizations, such as the Helsinki Commission, to weaken in order to create the necessity of a new order that is not predicated primarily on Western influence. Putin is rebuilding Russia's national identity through military action. This activity is hurting the basic freedoms and human rights of Russian citizens, as well as threatening Russia's contiguous neighbors and NATO members.

Recently, an American paramedic serving on the OSCE's Special Monitoring Mission in Ukraine was killed when his vehicle struck an explosive in separatist-held territory. This death was entirely preventable. Continued Russian military aggression in this region only increases the likelihood that more innocent lives will be taken. We must find a way to limit Russia's military aggression and bring balance back to the region.

PREPARED STATEMENT OF DR. MICHAEL CARPENTER, SENIOR DIRECTOR, PENN BIDEN
CENTER FOR DIPLOMACY AND GLOBAL ENGAGEMENT

Note: The statements, views, and policy recommendations expressed in this testimony reflect the opinions of the author alone, and do not necessarily reflect the positions of the Biden Center for Diplomacy and Global Engagement or the University of Pennsylvania.

Chairman Wicker, Co-Chairman Smith, and members of the Commission, thank you for this opportunity to speak with you today about the growing Russian military threat to European security.

There is no question that the Putin regime today poses the greatest threat to the security of Europe, and to the United States as well. Over the last decade, the Kremlin has repeatedly demonstrated a willingness to use military force to violate international norms and commitments. Russia's invasions of Georgia in 2008 and Ukraine in 2014 broke with the foundational principles of the postwar international order: sovereignty, territorial integrity, and the inviolability of borders. These principles were not only enshrined in the UN Charter and the Helsinki Final Act, which Moscow signed during the Soviet period, but they were also reaffirmed by Russia in the post-Cold War period in the Charter of Paris for a New Europe and the NATO-Russia Founding Act.

In addition to its brazen violations of international norms, the Kremlin is today in breach of several important arms control treaties that affect European security. In 2007, Russia unilaterally "suspended" its participation in the Conventional Forces in Europe Treaty, allowing Moscow to indirectly receive data provided by NATO countries (via its allies in the Collective Security Treaty Organization) without being required to reciprocate. Moreover, Moscow is covertly violating the Intermediate-Range Nuclear Forces (INF) Treaty by developing and likely soon deploying a prohibited ground-launched cruise missile. Finally, Russia is violating the Open Skies Treaty by restricting other states' ability to fly over Kaliningrad, a strategically important and heavily militarized outpost that borders on two NATO Allies.

When it comes to the Vienna Document and other transparency and confidence-building measures, Russia regularly undermines the spirit, if not the letter, of these arrangements. For example, the Russian General Staff often splits an exercise into several parts and/or creates artificial time-gaps between different parts of the exercise to bypass Vienna Document thresholds for notification and observation. Russia has also significantly increased the number of snap exercises—four in 2013, 8 in 2014, 20 in 2015, and 11 in 2016—that fall outside the scope of the Vienna Document's notification procedures. Finally, Russia continues to unilaterally block proposed updates to the Vienna Document that would lower the thresholds for inspections and evaluations, a step all other OSCE participating States strongly support.

Beyond the field of arms control, Russia has undermined a number of important political agreements affecting European security. These include the 1994 Budapest Memorandum, under which Ukraine gave up its nuclear weapons in return for a guarantee of its territorial integrity; the 2008 Medvedev-Sarkozy ceasefire agreement, under which Russia pledged to pull back its troops in Georgia to pre-conflict positions; and the September 2014 and February 2015 Minsk agreements whose ceasefire provisions are regularly violated, as demonstrated by the more than 80 Ukrainians killed and over 450 wounded this year alone (in total, almost 10,000 people have been killed in this conflict).

From its rampant abuse of Interpol "red warrants" to its disrespect for the fair competition standards of the International Olympic Committee, the Russian government has repeatedly demonstrated that its international commitments have almost no bearing on its behavior. Now is not the time to seek new commitments, but it is past time to take action so that Russia changes its behavior.

Russia's Collision Course with the West

To best understand how to address Russia's failure to honor its international commitments, we first need to understand what is motivating the Kremlin's behavior.

Put simply, the Putin regime believes the West poses the greatest threat to its survival and therefore seeks to push back against Western influence, including the spread of Western norms of transparency, accountability, and rule of law, which the Kremlin fears will undermine its kleptocratic and authoritarian system of rule. For much of the post-Cold War period this pushback was confined to the post-Soviet region, which Russian leaders referred to as their "sphere of privileged interests." In the last few years, however, the Kremlin has taken the fight directly to the West. On an increasing number of levels, the Kremlin is actively seeking to subvert the foundations of Western liberal democracies and to undermine NATO on its own turf, as we clearly saw through Russia's cyber-attack and subversive operation during our presidential election campaign. Indeed, Russia's foreign policy has undergone a significant paradigm shift in the last five years: from the previous model of cooperating where possible and competing where necessary, to the current model of competing short of conflict across all domains, all the time.

Recognizing that NATO possesses superior conventional military capabilities, Russia's "grey zone" conflict with the West relies primarily on unconventional tactics, unlike its conventional military interventions in Georgia and Ukraine. That is because Russia's leadership likely learned an important lesson from its wars in Georgia and Ukraine: namely, that while these conflicts set back both countries' Euro-Atlantic integration processes, neither of these interventions reversed the pro-Western orientations of their populations. As a result, the Kremlin now appears to be placing more emphasis on political subversion and covert influence operations, from Moldova to Montenegro and from Ukraine to the United States.

Investing in Full-Spectrum Capabilities

While Moscow has recognized that its competition with the West requires a greater emphasis on unconventional tactics, Russian military strategists continue to invest in the full range of conventional and nuclear capabilities to deter adversaries and prevail in active conflicts. The Russian General Staff has spent the last decade and a half implementing serious military reforms that have produced a far more ready and capable fighting force.

At the top end of the spectrum, Moscow is modernizing its nuclear triad: developing new ICBMs, advanced nuclear-powered submarines, and fifth-generation combat aircraft and new long-range bombers. In terms of conventional capabilities, Russia has fielded highly capable air and coastal defense systems for anti-access, area-denial (A2/AD) effects in Kaliningrad, Crimea, Japan's Northern Territories, and around large population centers like Moscow and St. Petersburg. It has developed and used sophisticated sea-launched cruise missiles. As we have seen in Ukraine, Russia has employed cutting-edge electronic warfare (EW) capabilities to suppress enemy Intelligence, Surveillance, and Reconnaissance (ISR) platforms while using its own EW-hardened ISR to target opposing forces with precision fire. Though using slightly older technology, Russia's conventional doctrine also calls for extensive and highly effective use of multiple rocket launch systems and artillery, which have together accounted for more than 90 percent of the casualties in Ukraine. Finally, on the covert end of the spectrum, Russia has honed a variety of unconventional capabilities that include cutting-edge cyber, proxy, and information warfare, as well as the weaponization of corruption for purposes of political subversion.

Cultivating Belligerence, Unpredictability, and Non-Transparency

Russia relies on its status as a nuclear power to deter and instill fear of escalation among its adversaries. Russia's "escalate to de-escalate" doctrine allows for first use of a nuclear weapon to compel adversaries to settle a conflict on Moscow's terms rather than to fight on or escalate the conflict. Under this doctrine Russia could, for example, use a tactical nuclear weapon for a first-use "demonstration effect." If used in a conflict with a NATO Ally, however, this could have the exact opposite of its intended effect and prove dangerously escalatory, with devastating consequences for all parties. The Trump administration would therefore do well to consider a new round of strategic stability talks with Russia to bring to Russia's attention such doctrinal miscalculations.

Another goal of Russia's evolving military doctrine is to use denial, deception, unpredictability, and lack of transparency to maximize Russia's asymmetric tactical advantages. The Kremlin's numerous violations of arms control and confidence- and security-building measures (CSBMs) are therefore part of a very deliberate strategy, and one that takes full advantage of the clear asymmetry in the desire for transparency between Russia and Europe.

This deliberate erosion of transparency and trust on Russia's part is coupled with nuclear threats against NATO Allies and dangerous military behavior whose purpose is to intimidate. The threats to target Denmark or Romania with nuclear weapons and the highly unprofessional and unsafe intercepts of NATO aircraft and vessels over/on the Black and Baltic seas fall into this category. Earlier this month, for example, a Russian fighter intercepted a U.S. P-8A aircraft flying over the Black Sea at a distance of only 20 feet, endangering the lives of both American and Russian aircrews. While these dangerous activities have led some European countries to recommend new crisis management measures such as an agreement to keep transponders on at all times, such proposals completely miss the point. Transponders or new navigational rules will do nothing to solve the problem because these incidents are not accidents resulting from the excessive bravado of individual pilots. They are deliberate policy choices and will continue so long as Moscow thinks it can intimidate NATO countries into scaling back their operations in certain theaters, such as the Black and Baltic seas.

Policies to Respond to an Aggressive Russia

The range of aggressive and subversive actions that Russia is pursuing across Europe demands a firm but proportionate response. Given Russia's ongoing violations of the fundamental principles of the NATO-Russia Founding Act, the United States should finally consider unilaterally declaring a "suspension" of its pledge not to deploy "substantial combat forces" to NATO Allies in Eastern and Central Europe. The current situation in which Russia violates almost every one of its Founding Act pledges while NATO meekly declares its continued compliance with the Act—and thereby creates a "second-class" status for our eastern Allies—creates an incentive for the additional buildup of Russian troops on its western border. To compensate for this imbalance, the United States should deploy an additional Brigade Combat Team to Eastern Europe as a deterrent force, while clearly messaging that this deployment could be reversed if and when Russia's aggressive posture in the region changes. At the same time, the United States should declare that for now it is reaffirming its commitment to the Founding Act's three "nuclear no's," namely the commitment that NATO has "no intention, no plan, and no reason" to deploy nuclear weapons to the eastern flank of the Alliance.

Second, the United States must signal that it will employ the legal principle of countermeasures to respond to Russia's violations of the Open Skies and INF treaties. Just as Russia denies access under the Open Skies Treaty to the exclave of Kaliningrad, the United States should immediately choose an analogous region (e.g. Hawaii or Alaska) where it can mirror Russian restrictions until Moscow returns to compliance with the treaty. The Departments of State and Defense should also more forthrightly communicate to our Allies our concern with Russia's ability to use the Open Skies Treaty to collect information on NATO's critical infrastructure. Although many of our Allies greatly value the transparency the treaty provides, in many respects this transparency is of marginal benefit to the United States. Our Allies must therefore understand that the risks to U.S. national security inherent in the intrusive treaty procedures are beginning to outweigh its benefits.

Similarly, the United States has spent considerable time seeking unsuccessfully to convince Moscow to return to compliance with the INF treaty. It is now time for the United States to apply the doctrine of countermeasures to immediately begin research (which is not prohibited by the treaty) into the development of an intermediate-range missile that would match Russia's new capability. The Pentagon should also be tasked with implementing other defensive measures to deny Russia any advantage from its violation of the treaty. Finally, we must also accelerate our diplomatic efforts with Allies to underscore that the United States cannot continue to stand by indefinitely as Russia develops a new and extremely dangerous military capability.

Third, strengthening Ukraine's sovereignty must be a central element of the U.S. response to Russian aggression in Europe. The current de facto arms embargo on Ukraine should be lifted immediately and defensive armaments should be provided to allow Ukraine to harden its defenses against further Russian aggression. U.S. security assistance should focus on air defense, anti-armor, and counter-artillery/mortar capabilities as well as more robust intelligence sharing. If the United States took the lead, a number of our NATO Allies would almost certainly follow suit and send excess stocks of non-NATO standard weapons to Ukraine to make up for the losses that Ukraine has sustained during the war.

The United States must also insist on joining France and Germany in the "Normandy format" negotiations between Russia and Ukraine in order to participate in the development of a detailed roadmap with concrete timelines for implementing the Minsk agreements. The United States must be prepared to back up such a roadmap with concrete consequences for Russia's failure to implement the necessary steps, for example by unilaterally applying blocking sanctions on select Russian financial institutions. U.S. and EU sanctions have so far been too blunt of an instrument to affect incremental policy decisions because they have not been tied to any specific benchmarks other than the full implementation of the Minsk agreement, for which they are too weak to shift the Kremlin's calculus. Full blocking sanctions on select Russian financial institutions would have an immediate and significant effect even if the U.S. were to apply them unilaterally, and could help incentivize Moscow's withdrawal of troops from the Donbas if calibrated to match appropriate benchmarks for the implementation of the Minsk agreements.

In the near term, the United States should also seek to upgrade the OSCE Special Monitoring Mission in Ukraine or even consider the creation of an armed UN mission. Following the April 23 killing of an American OSCE monitor with a roadside mine, the OSCE has significantly cut back its patrols in the separatist-controlled areas. These unarmed patrols were never properly outfitted for the mandate they were given and from the very start monitors have only been able to patrol during daylight hours. The personnel of the Special Monitoring Mission have performed heroically under these circumstances and have repeatedly taken on enormous personal risks to monitor compliance with the Minsk agreements. However, the current situation is no longer tenable. The OSCE Structured Dialogue on European security should take up the issue of a larger and more robust monitoring mission as a matter of precedence and urgency.

Responding to Russia's Cyber-Attacks on the West

In response to the cyber-attacks and information warfare that the Kremlin has perpetrated against the United States and other Western democracies, the United States must rally its Allies to impose serious consequences for Russia's aggressive behavior. The response thus far has been weak and ineffectual. The declaration of 35 Russian officials as *persona non grata* and the prohibition on Russian use of intelligence gathering facilities in the United States is a mere slap on the wrist and does not serve as a deterrent against future cyber-attacks.

Given reports of Russia's extensive penetration of U.S. and Allied government networks, the United States must invest significantly more resources in cyber defense. Most importantly, Congress should legislate regulations to force the private sector companies that control our critical infrastructure to adopt a common set of cyber defense standards. As last week's ransomware attack demonstrates, the private sector networks that run our critical infrastructure are extremely vulnerable. The Pentagon should also increase its support for cyber defense of our most vulnerable Allies.

Finally, the United States must immediately appoint an independent Special Prosecutor to determine whether or not there was collusion or cooperation between the Russian government and campaign representatives in the last U.S. presidential election cycle. It must also establish a Select Committee to look at the broader question of Russian interference in the U.S. electoral process and Russia's ability to penetrate our critical infrastructure networks. The failure to take these steps damages not just U.S. national security but also transatlantic security. If the Kremlin's successful execution of one of the most audacious subversive operations in history is not immediately countered, it will only embolden Russia to take similar actions in the future.

Conclusion

Chairman Wicker, Co-Chairman Smith, and members of the Commission, the United States has not only a role to play, but an obligation to enhance deterrence and build resilience against Russian aggression and malign influence across the entire OSCE region from Vancouver to Vladivostok. It starts here at home, by taking Russia's subversive actions against the United States seriously and deploying the necessary tools to expose them and respond with the imposition of proportionate costs. We must also push back on Russia's violations of arms control and confidence-building agreements by implementing necessary countermeasures and denying Russia any advantage. Finally, we must get more actively involved in finding a solution to the Ukraine conflict by applying greater leverage against Moscow and strengthening Ukraine's defenses. The best disincentive for any future aggression against our partners and Allies is for the aggressor to finally understand that in the end the costs will outweigh the benefits.

Chairman Wicker, Co-Chairman Smith, other members of the Commission, thank you for inviting me to testify at this hearing on the Russian military threat in Europe.

I understand that my co-panelists will speak to Russian military actions in recent years that have seriously degraded the security environment in Europe—the Ukraine conflict in particular—and the role the OSCE can play in restoring security and trust in the region. I have been asked to assess Russia's record of compliance with the arms control and confidence-building agreements that are particularly relevant to security in Europe, including the Conventional Armed Forces in Europe (CFE) Treaty of 1990, the Open Skies Treaty of 1992, the Vienna Document on Confidence- and Security-Building Measures, originally adopted in 1990 and updated most recently in 2011, and the Intermediate-Range Nuclear Forces (INF) Treaty of 1987.

I will briefly review the obligations arising under each of these agreements and discuss the degree to which Russia is currently living up to its obligations. I will then draw some overall conclusions about Russia's approach to these agreements, and the implications for the United States and our allies.

CFE Treaty

The CFE Treaty was concluded in 1990 and entered into force in November 1992. It included as states party all members of NATO and the Warsaw Pact. For all of these states party, it imposed strict limits on the amounts of specified military hardware (called "Treaty-Limited Equipment" or "TLE") that they could deploy in specified areas in the treaty's area of application, which stretches from the Atlantic Ocean to the Ural Mountains. Following the treaty's entry into force, over 52,000 pieces of TLE were destroyed or converted by the United States, Russia, and other states party to the treaty.

Underlying the treaty was the belief that the imbalance in conventional armed forces in Europe (which favored the Soviet Union and the Warsaw Pact during the Cold War) had created instability and fear on the Continent, and led NATO to rely increasingly on its nuclear deterrent. The concept of the treaty was that if this conventional imbalance could be eliminated, stability could be restored, and reliance on nuclear weapons diminished. In this sense, the CFE Treaty sought to ameliorate one of the principal causes of the nuclear arms race that emerged during the Cold War, and it provided a foundation for the dramatic reductions in strategic nuclear arms levels that have been negotiated between the United States and Russia following the end of the Cold War.

Regrettably, in July 2007, President Putin ordered a "suspension" of Russian implementation of the treaty. The other states party have not recognized this suspension as a legally permissible step, and therefore all the other parties have continued to observe the treaty as between them. In 2011, however, the United States and its NATO allies (plus Georgia and Moldova) bowed to reality and accepted that Russia was not going to permit verification inspections under the treaty to take place on Russian territory. Accordingly, they ceased requesting inspections on Russian territory, and declared that they would cease implementation of their obligations to Russia.

From the moment the treaty entered into force in November 1992, the Russian military deployments in Georgia and Moldova violated Article IV, paragraph 5 of the treaty, which prohibits a state party from stationing its "conventional armed forces on the territory of another State Party without the agreement of that State Party." Russia's 2014 military intervention in Ukraine compounded its non-compliance with this basic provision of the CFE Treaty. Russia is today stationing its conventional armed forces on the territory of not just two, but now three states party, without the consent of those states party, in violation of Article IV, paragraph 5 of the treaty.

The United States has tried hard since 2007 to persuade Russia to return to compliance with the treaty, but to no avail. The fundamental problem is that Russia concluded more than a decade ago that the CFE Treaty was no longer serving its interests. Among other things, Moscow chafed at the treaty's so-called Flank Limits, which it believed constrained its ability to carry out military operations on Russia's periphery, for example, in Chechnya. Moscow was also unhappy that Georgia and Moldova were using the treaty to pressure Russia to withdraw unwelcome Russian forces from their territory. Following the Russian military intervention in Ukraine in 2014, Russia is now violating Article IV, paragraph 5 of the treaty in three states party, further diminishing the likelihood that it will return to compliance with the treaty.

Open Skies Treaty

The Open Skies Treaty was signed in 1992, and created a regime for the conduct of observation flights over the territory of other states party. These flights use photography and other sensors to collect information about activities on the ground in the countries being observed. The collection of this information is intended as a confidence-building measure among the parties. There are today 34 states party to the treaty, including the United States and Russia.

Russia has continued to implement the Open Skies Treaty, but has unilaterally imposed restrictions on the conduct of observation flights over its territory that are legally inconsistent with the treaty and clearly intended to diminish the benefits of the treaty to the other states party.

Perhaps most significantly for the United States, Russia has arbitrarily imposed a sublimit of 500 kilometers on the distance of observation flights out of one of its Open Skies airfields with respect to observation flights over the Kaliningrad Oblast. There is no legal basis in the treaty for imposing such a sublimit, and all other observation flights out of that airfield are subject to the treaty's standard distance limitation of 5500 kilometers. The practical consequence of this restriction is not to prevent observation of the Kaliningrad Oblast, but to require multiple flights to be able to observe the entire territory of that Oblast. This is, therefore, a legally ill-founded nuisance restriction aimed at discouraging observation of a piece of Russian territory that is of great interest to NATO, sandwiched as it is between NATO members Poland and Lithuania.

Other examples of ill-founded Russian restrictions include:

- Minimum altitude restrictions—Russia imposes a minimum altitude restriction on observation flights over Moscow that limit the amount of data that can be collected. It previously imposed a similar restriction on flights over Chechnya, but lifted this restriction in early 2016.
- Restrictions on flights adjacent to Abkhazia and South Ossetia—Russia prohibits observation flights within 10 kilometers of its border with the Georgian regions of Abkhazia and South Ossetia.
- Improper invocation of *force majeure*—Russia has on occasion improperly invoked the concept of *force majeure* to make changes to observation flight routes, ostensibly due to "VIP movements."

In addition, Russia has arbitrarily imposed a restriction on exercise by Ukraine of its rights under the treaty. The treaty entitles countries hosting observation flights to charge observing countries for such things as fuel, de-icing fluid, and ground and technical services for their aircraft, and the treaty provides a mechanism for submitting invoices for such costs and settling accounts at the end of each calendar year. In the case of Ukraine, however, Russia has insisted on payment in advance before any observation flight by Ukrainian aircraft from a Russian airfield. As a consequence, Ukraine's last solo observation flight over Russia was in 2014. Meanwhile Ukraine has conducted 20 observation flights over other states party since 2014 with no issues in payment.

Despite these problems, it should be noted that observation flights have continued over Russia, including the first-ever "Extraordinary Observation Flight," requested by Ukraine pursuant to the treaty shortly after Russia's intervention in the Crimea, and carried out using a U.S. aircraft.

Overall, therefore, while Russia continues to observe the Open Skies Treaty, it often does not do so in the full spirit of transparency that the treaty was intended to promote.

Vienna Document

The Vienna Document on Confidence- and Security-Building Measures was first adopted under the auspices of the OSCE in 1990, and updated in 1992, 1994, 1999, and most recently in 2011. As with all previous versions of the Vienna Document, the latest version, Vienna Document 2011 (VD11), is not a treaty, but rather an agreed set of transparency measures that all members of the OSCE have agreed to implement in order to increase confidence within the OSCE region. Among these measures are data exchanges, inspections, and notifications of certain military activities.

The State Department's annual arms control compliance report for 2016, released just last month, stated the following about Russia's compliance with VD11:

> The United States assesses that the Russian Federation's … selective implementation of certain provisions of VD11 and the resultant loss of transparency about Russian military activities has limited the effectiveness of the CSBMs regime. Russia's selective implementation also raises concerns as to Russia's adherence to VD11.

The report goes on to detail a number of ways in which Russia's behavior falls short of its obligations under VD11. These include:

- Russia's continued occupation and claimed annexation of Crimea, and support to and fighting with separatists in Eastern Ukraine, violates paragraph 3 of VD11, which reaffirmed Russia's commitment to refrain from the threat or use of force.
- Russia has failed to provide information on its military forces located in the Georgian regions of Abkhazia and South Ossetia, as well as on two Russian units located in Crimea.
- Russia has established a pattern of conducting military exercises without properly notifying them as required under VD11, ostensibly because they are "snap exercises," or because it claims they are multiple activities under separate command, when to all appearances they are large-scale activities under unitary command. In a recent case in August 2016, Russia conducted an exercise involving over 100,000 personnel, but only provided advance notice of an exercise involving 12,600 personnel.
- Russia has failed to provide data of several types of military equipment that is obligated to report under VD11, including the BRM-1K armored combat vehicle, the Su-30SM multirole fighter, and the Ka-52 attack helicopter.

Further, Russia has in the past defied efforts by other parties to the Vienna Document to invoke the agreement's mechanism for consultations in the event of unusual military activities. When this mechanism was invoked with respect to Russia's activities involving Ukraine, Russia either failed to provide responsive replies to requests for an explanation of the activities, or, in some cases, boycotted meetings called to discuss the activities.

Russia continues to permit other VD11 inspections and evaluations to take place on its territory, and continues to participate in data exchanges. But Russia's reporting practices—particularly with regard to the notification of military exercises—have given rise to suspicions that, at best, Russia is structuring its activities to evade VD11 reporting requirements, or, at worst, misrepresenting those activities in order to justify not reporting them. Its selective implementation of VD11 is contrary to the spirit of the agreement, and has diminished rather enhanced confidence among members of the OSCE.

INF Treaty

The INF Treaty was concluded in 1987, and committed the United States and the Soviet Union to neither possess, produce, nor flight-test ground-launched missiles with maximum ranges between 500 and 5500 kilometers. Pursuant to the treaty, by May of 1991, the United States eliminated approximately 800 INF-range missiles and the Soviet Union eliminated approximately 1800 such missiles.

Negotiated at the height of the Cold War, the INF Treaty contributed to security in the European theater, and was profoundly reassuring to the populations of some of our key NATO allies. It was in many ways a vindication of President Reagan's policy of promoting "peace through strength."

The Obama Administration announced in July of 2014 that it had "determined that the Russian Federation is in violation of its obligations under the INF Treaty not to possess, produce, or flight-test a ground-launched cruise missile (GLCM) with a range capability of 500 km to 5,500 km, or to possess or produce launchers of such missiles." The State Department's annual arms control compliance report for 2016, released just last month, reaffirmed that "the Russian Federation continued to be in violation of its obligations under the INF Treaty." Substantially similar language was included in the State Department's arms control compliance reports published in 2014, 2015 and 2016.

The Obama and Trump Administrations have been somewhat cryptic in describing the precise nature of the Russian violation, due apparently to the need to protect intelligence sources and methods. According to reports that have appeared in the New York Times and Washington Post, the violation involves a new type of ground-launched cruise missile called the SSC-8, with a range between 500 and

5500 kilometers. When the Obama Administration first announced the violation in 2014, the missile reportedly had been flight-tested, but not yet deployed. Press reporting in February of this year claimed that the missile has now been operationally deployed and is in the possession of two Russian battalions. And while the Obama Administration only formally determined in 2014 that Russia was violating the treaty, it appears that the Obama Administration first came to suspect that Russia was violating the treaty in 2011, and the first test of this missile may have taken place several years earlier.

The Obama and Trump Administrations have attempted to have a dialogue with Russia about correcting the violation of the treaty. This has been a sterile dialogue, however, with Russia professing not to even know what missile the United States is complaining about. This despite the fact that the United States has provided detailed information to Russia about the missile, including Russia's internal designator for the mobile launcher chassis, the names of the companies involved in developing and producing the missile and launcher, and the missile's test history, including the coordinates of the tests. So long as Russia persists in denying the existence of the missile in question, there appears to be little hope of resolving the violation.

As with the CFE Treaty, Russia has long been unhappy living under the restrictions of the INF Treaty. The basic Russian complaint is that the treaty applies only to the United States and four successor states to the Soviet Union (including Russia), and therefore leaves every other country in the world free to produce and deploy INF-range missiles. Increasingly other countries are doing precisely that, including many countries located within striking distance of Russia, such as China, Iran, North Korea and Pakistan.

It is a sad irony, of course, that missile technology proliferation from Russia contributed significantly to the missile programs of Iran and North Korea, and that North Korea in turn contributed to Pakistan's missile program. So in fact, Russia's complaint is in significant part of its own making.

As early as 2005, Russian Defense Minister Sergei Ivanov raised with Secretary of Defense Donald Rumsfeld the possibility of Russian withdrawal from the treaty. President Putin lamented in 2013 that "nearly all of our neighbors are developing these kinds of weapons systems," and asserted that the decision to sign the treaty was "debatable to say the least." I know from my own conversations with Russian officials during my time in government that they would like to get out from under the INF Treaty.

Certainly this underlying unhappiness with the INF treaty helps explain why Russia has been willing to violate it. In discussing how to respond to this violation, we need to recognize that Moscow would welcome a decision by the United States to terminate the treaty, because that would relieve them of the need at some point to do so. The Obama Administration's decision to leave the INF treaty in place despite Russia's testing of a missile prohibited under the treaty was no doubt motivated, at least in part, by a desire not to reward Russia for its violation. However, as the nature of the violation has shifted from testing a prohibited missile to operationally deploying that missile, the United States will find it increasingly hard to overlook the violation.

Concluding Observations

A clear pattern emerges when one looks at Russia's implementation of its arms control obligations overall. Moscow will comply with such agreements so long as it judges them to be in Russia's interest. But to the degree Moscow concludes such agreements have ceased to serve its interest, it will seek to terminate them (CFE Treaty), violate them while continuing to pay them lip service (INF Treaty), or selectively implement them (Open Skies Treaty and Vienna Document).

Such actions are, of course, destructive to the sense of confidence and security that CSBMs are intended to promote. But Russia believes that this is how great powers are entitled to act, and today Moscow insists on acting and being respected as a great power.

The underlying problem appears to be the Russian leadership's belief that security in Europe is a zero-sum game; that gains in the security of Russia's neighbors can only come at the expense of Russian security, and that Russia can improve its security by diminishing the security of its neighbors. This mindset is, of course, completely contrary to the premise of the existing arms control and CSBM architecture of Europe, which holds that security in Europe is a positive-sum game, and that all countries will be more secure to the degree their neighbors are also more secure.

We have a new President who came to office determined to work out a new and more positive relationship with Russia. He appears to believe—correctly in my view—that there are no fundamental conflicts between America's vital national interests and Russia's. The greatest challenges to both of us are the same, including the threats of jihadism and a rising China that increasingly sees itself as a hegemon in Asia, if not beyond. Indeed, one could argue that, comparing Russia's geography to our own, these are even greater threats to Russia than to the United States.

Viewed through the prism of core national interests, it is indeed a great tragedy that the United States has been unable to establish a stronger security partnership with Russia since the end of the Cold War. We can content ourselves that the fault for this lies much more on the Russian side than on our side, but pointing fingers does not move us closer to building the kind of partnership our shared core interests suggest we should have. So it is my hope that President Trump succeeds in persuading the Russian leadership that security in Europe is in fact a positive sum game, and that Russia will be safer and more secure to the degree its immediate neighbors in Europe are also more secure.

Whether it happens during the Trump Administration, or at some point further in the future, I am confident that Russia eventually will discover that its true national interests lie in cooperating with the other members of the OSCE rather than seeking to intimidate them. Until that time comes, however, we must be clear-eyed about the challenges we face. We have to deal with Russia as it is, rather than how we wish it to be.

I thank you for holding this hearing, and look forward to responding to your questions.

PREPARED STATEMENT OF AMBASSADOR STEPHEN PIFER, SENIOR FELLOW AND DIRECTOR OF THE ARMS CONTROL AND NON-PROLIFERATION INITIATIVE, THE BROOKINGS INSTITUTION

The Growing Russian Military Threat in Europe-Assessing and Addressing the Challenge: The Case of Ukraine

Introduction

Mr. Chairman, Co-Chairman Smith, members of the Commission, thank you for the opportunity to appear today to testify on the growing Russian military threat to Europe and how that threat has manifested itself in Ukraine.

From the perspective of the 1975 Helsinki Final Act, Russia's military aggression against Ukraine has been the most shocking development in Europe since the end of the Cold War and collapse of the Soviet Union. The Russian seizure of Crimea in March 2014, followed by its illegal annexation, violated fundamental principles of the Final Act. Those principles include the commitment of participating states to respect each other's sovereignty, territorial integrity and independence, and to refrain from the threat or use of force against the territorial integrity or independence of any state. The principles also include the principle that borders can be changed only by peaceful means and agreement. Russia's actions in Crimea have violated all of those commitments.

The Kremlin did not stop with Crimea. Russia military and security service personnel have been deeply engaged in the Donbas region of eastern Ukraine since April 2014, where fighting has claimed some 10,000 lives. Russian involvement in the Donbas has included the provision of leadership, financing, ammunition, heavy weapons, supplies and, in some cases, regular units of the Russian army to support armed separatism against the Ukrainian government, also in violation of Russia's Final Act commitments.

Unfortunately, and despite the efforts of the leaders of Germany and France, the conflict in Donbas shows no sign of settlement. There is little evidence to suggest that Russia and the separatist forces under its control want to end the conflict. The Kremlin appears to see value in maintaining a simmering conflict as a means to put pressure on and destabilize the government in Kyiv, in order to make it harder for Ukraine to get on with needed domestic reforms and implement its association agreement with the European Union.

It is important for European security that the United States and the West support Ukraine and stand up to Russia. It would be a mistake to let the Kremlin conclude that the kind of tactics it has employed against Ukraine could be applied elsewhere against another member of the Organization for Security and Cooperation in Europe (OSCE).

Russia's Goals in Europe and Ukraine

In the 1990s and early 2000s, many analysts assumed that Russia wanted to work in a cooperative manner with the United States and Europe and, if not integrate into, develop cooperative relationships with key European and trans-Atlantic institutions such as the European Union and NATO. In recent years, however, it has become clear that Russian President Vladimir Putin and the Kremlin leadership have chosen a different course. They appear to have concluded that the European security order that developed in the aftermath of the Cold War disadvantages Russian interests. They have sought to undermine that order and define Russia in opposition to the United States and the West.

Russia is pursuing several goals in Europe. First, the Kremlin seeks a Russian sphere of influence—or a "sphere of privileged interests," as then-President Dmitry Medvedev called it in 2008—in the post-Soviet space, with the possible exception of the Baltic States. Mr. Putin does not seek to recreate the Soviet Union, as the Russian economy is not prepared to subsidize the economies of the other former Soviet states. What the Russian leadership wants from its neighbors is that they defer to Moscow on issues that the Kremlin defines as key to Russian interests. This includes relationships between those states and institutions such as the European Union and NATO, despite Russia's commitment under the Final Act to respect the right of other states to choose to belong to international organizations and to be party to treaties of alliance.

Second, Moscow seeks to weaken the European Union and NATO, which it believes act as checks on Russian power. Russian security doctrine openly regards NATO as a threat. Mr. Putin appears to hold a particular grievance against NATO. He asserts that the Alliance began enlarging in the early 1990s in order to take advantage of Russian weakness and bring military force to Russia's borders. His narrative ignores NATO's efforts to engage Russia in a cooperative manner as well as the commitments undertaken by the Alliance with regard to the non-stationing of nuclear and conventional forces on the territory of new member states, commitments made to ease Russian concern about NATO enlargement.

The Kremlin also regards the European Union and its enlargement as a threat. Indeed, the Russian pressure that began on Ukraine in 2013 was not due to that country's relationship with NATO. Then-President Victor Yanukovych had renounced the goal of securing a NATO membership action plan, and key Alliance members such as Germany and France had made clear that they did not support putting Ukraine on a membership track. What spurred Russia to increase its pressure was the prospect that Ukraine—even under Mr. Yanukovych—might conclude an association agreement with the European Union.

Third, the Kremlin seeks a seat at the table when major questions regarding Europe are decided. This explains in part Russia's opposition to the European Union and NATO; Russia does not belong to those institutions. While Russia is a member of OSCE, it has devalued the status of the organization over the past two decades, regularly calling into question its mission and, at times, even its legitimacy.

Russia's more assertive and belligerent stance in Europe over the past five years has been abetted by the modernization of Russian military forces, both nuclear and conventional. Much of the modernization of Russian strategic nuclear forces appears to be replacing old weapons systems with new versions—in some cases, systems Moscow might have replaced years ago had it then had the finances. The overall strategic modernization program appears sized to fit within the limits of the 2010 New Strategic Arms Reduction Treaty.

More worrisome, particularly for European security, are Russia's deployment of a new ground-launched intermediate-range cruise missile in violation of the 1987 Intermediate-range Nuclear Forces Treaty, its modernization of an array of other non-strategic nuclear weapons, and its apparent "escalate to de-escalate" doctrine. Formal Russian doctrine suggests that Russia would resort to use of nuclear weapons in the event that nuclear or other weapons of mass destruction were used against Russia or an ally, or in the event of a conventional attack on Russia in which the existence of the Russian state is at stake. There have, however, been suggestions that Moscow might entertain the notion that it could use nuclear weapons to "de-escalate" a conventional conflict that did not involve an attack on Russian territory, for example, after a Russian conventional attack on another country.

Russia is also modernizing its conventional military forces. While much of this appears to be replacing old with new, the Russian military clearly aims to enhance its ability to conduct offensive operations outside of Russian territory, spurred in part by a desire to improve on the mediocre performance of Russian forces in the 2008 Georgia-Russia conflict. Over the past three years, it appears that Russia has deployed and operated a number of its new conventional weapons systems in Ukraine.

Domestic Drivers of Russian Policy toward Ukraine

Domestic political factors constitute major drivers of Russian policy toward Ukraine. For the Kremlin, regime preservation is job number one. During his first two terms as president in 2000-2008, Mr. Putin based regime legitimacy on economics—at a time when the Russian economy was growing at a rate of about seven percent per year. However, when he prepared to return to the presidency in 2011, Russia faced a grim economic situation. Accordingly, Mr. Putin included heavy elements of nationalism, Russia's return as a great power, and anti-Americanism in his campaign. Those themes now appear the basis for regime legitimacy, and it is likely that they will feature in Mr. Putin's campaign for reelection in March 2018.

Those themes in turn drive aspects of Moscow's foreign policy, and they play in particular with regard to Ukraine. From 1654 until 1991, Ukraine was a part of the Russian Empire and then the Soviet Union, with the exception of a few years after World War I. Of all the republics that Moscow lost when the Soviet Union collapsed, Ukraine's loss pains Russians the most. Many Russians consider Ukraine "little Russia." Indeed, when he made his last visit to Kyiv in summer 2013, Mr. Putin referred to Russians and Ukrainians as one people—to the unhappiness of many Ukrainians, who felt that he thereby denied their history, language and culture.

Mr. Putin, moreover, appears to fear that a successful Ukraine could affect the attitudes of the Russian people. If Ukraine succeeds in building a stable, modern, democratic state with a robust market economy, Russians may begin to wonder why they cannot have a more democratic form of governance in place of the increasingly authoritarian power structure that has developed in Russia over the past seventeen years. While Mr. Putin enjoys high approval ratings—typically in the 70-80 percent range—the Kremlin seems constantly nervous about its hold on the Russian public. The Kremlin thus does not want a successful Ukrainian neighbor and is prepared to go to great lengths to hinder that success, including the use of military force.

The Maydan and Russia's Illegal Seizure of Crimea

In February 2014, the violent end of the Maydan Revolution, Mr. Yanukovych's decision to flee Kyiv, and the Rada (Ukraine's parliament) vote to appoint an acting president and acting prime minister who made drawing closer to the European Union Ukraine's top foreign policy priority caught Moscow by surprise. The Kremlin reacted quickly.

Mr. Putin told a Russian documentary a year later that he decided early on the morning of February 23 to activate a plan to seize the Crimean peninsula. Shortly thereafter, soldiers in Russian-style combat fatigues—but lacking identifying insignia—began to occupy key installations and crossroads on the peninsula. The soldiers were clearly professional military, as evidenced by how they handled their weapons and themselves.

Ukrainians dubbed these soldiers "little green men." Asked on March 4 whether the soldiers were Russian, Mr. Putin denied they were, describing them as "local self-defense forces." Asked about their Russian combat fatigues, he replied that one could find those in military surplus stores across the former Soviet Union. On March 28, however, Mr. Putin congratulated Russian military officers on their conduct of the Crimean operation. In a May 18 telethon, he admitted that the "little green men" had been Russian soldiers. The Ministry of Defense issued a medallion commemorating the Russian military's role in the "return of Crimea," an operation which the medallion dated as running from February 20 (three days before Mr. Putin said he ordered Crimea's seizure) through March 18.

Russia's swift seizure of Crimea was aided particularly by two factors. First, there were already substantial Russian military forces and infrastructure on the peninsula, deployed there per agreement with Ukraine at bases and facilities for the Russian Black Sea Fleet and supporting units. Second, Ukrainian military forces stayed in garrison and did not challenge the Russians, reportedly in part due to urgings from Washington that Ukraine do nothing to provoke Russian escalation. As many soldiers in the Ukrainian units were from Crimea, commanders likely had questions about their unit's reliability.

By March 6, Russian forces had control of all major locations in Crimea, had blocked Ukrainian forces in their bases, and had laid a minefield to cordon off the peninsula from the Ukrainian mainland. Under the leadership of a newly appointed prime minister who reportedly was once known as the "Goblin" in local organized crime circles, the Crimean parliament voted to join Russia and to schedule a referendum. That referendum, conducted on March 16, offered two choices: to join Russia, or to reinstate Crimea's 1992 constitution, which would have granted the peninsula substantially greater autonomy from Kyiv. Those who wanted Crimea to remain a part of Ukraine under the existing constitutional arrangement found no box to check.

Crimean authorities reported that 83 percent of eligible voters took part in the referendum, with nearly 97 percent voting to join Russia. Few found the result credible. There were numerous reports of irregularities, armed personnel near voting stations, and journalists with Russian passports allowed to vote. Other estimates indicated a much smaller voter turnout than that reported by Crimean and Russian officials. According to a report that appeared later on the website of the Russian president's human rights ombudsman, only 30-50 percent of the Crimean electorate actually took part in the referendum, with only 50-60 percent of those choosing to join Russia.

In any event, Crimean representatives and Russian officials two days later concluded a treaty on Crimea joining Russia. The Russian Federal Assembly ratified the treaty on March 21. The annexation of Crimea proved very popular with the Russian public, and it gave a boost to Mr. Putin's approval rating. He apparently remembers that; the 2018 presidential election in Russia has been scheduled for March 18, the fourth anniversary of the treaty on Crimea joining Russia.

The United States and European Union responded to Crimea's illegal annexation by applying visa and financial sanctions on individuals connected to the seizure. The leaders of the United States, Canada, France, Germany, Italy, Japan and United Kingdom agreed to exclude Russia from the G8 and revert to the G7. President Barack Obama signed an executive order to enable broader sanctions against the energy, financial and defense sectors of the Russian economy.

Russia's Involvement in the Donbas

Russia did not stop with Crimea. In early April 2014, "little green men" appeared along with armed local separatists in several major cities in eastern Ukraine, particularly in the Donbas region of Donetsk and Luhansk. In contrast to Crimea, this time Ukrainian security forces resisted, and fighting broke out in several locations.

The U.S., Russian and Ukrainian foreign ministers, joined by the European Union's high representative for common foreign and security policy, met in Geneva on April 17 and agreed on a settlement that called for an end to the violence, the disarming of illegal armed groups, and the evacuation of occupied public buildings. The settlement also called on OSCE to monitor the agreed measures. Separatist leaders in Donbas, however, immediately indicated that they would not observe the Geneva terms.

The fighting continued and spread, with the separatist forces gaining control of more of the Donbas. Russia provided leadership, financing, ammunition, heavy weapons and other supplies. In addition, "political tourists" began arriving from Russia to swell the ranks of the separatist fighters. While the separatists at first claimed they got their heavy weapons by seizing them from Ukrainian forces, equipment showed up in their ranks that had never been in the Ukrainian military's inventory but was in the Russian military's inventory.

The United States began to impose additional sanctions on Russia, as fighting in the Donbas continued and spread further. On the battlefield, however, Ukrainian forces began to gain the upper hand during the early summer. Russia responded by accelerating the flow of tanks, armored personnel carriers, artillery, advanced anti-aircraft systems and "volunteers" to assist the separatists.

The anti-aircraft systems provided by Russia included the Buk (SA-11) surface-to-air missile that shot down a Malaysia Airlines Boeing 777 on July 17 over the occupied part of the Donbas. All of the nearly 300 passengers and crew perished. A separatist leader almost immediately claimed credit for downing a Ukrainian military transport plane at the same time and location of the Malaysia Airlines shootdown. It appears that the separatist forces fired on the civilian airliner by mistake. Reports and photos that were issued later tracked the Buk missile launcher through territory occupied by the separatists, including the transport of the launcher—minus one missile—back in the direction of Russia.

In the aftermath of the shootdown, the United States and European Union adopted substantial new sanctions against Russia. These included sanctions aimed at the financial, energy, high tech and defense sectors.

Ukrainian forces continued to make progress. By mid-August, they had greatly reduced the amount of territory under Russian/separatist control, had split that territory into two pockets, and appeared on the verge of regaining control of all of the Donbas. On or about August 23, however, regular units of the Russian army, supported by heavy artillery and rocket strikes, entered Ukrainian territory and dealt a severe blow to Ukrainian forces. They inflicted heavy casualties on the Ukrainians and, by some estimates, destroyed 50-70 percent of the armor deployed in the area by the Ukrainian army. The Russian/separatist attack recovered much of the territory that had been lost in the two previous months.

Ukrainian representatives met with officials of the so-called Donetsk and Luhansk "people's republics" in Minsk on September 5 and worked out a ceasefire in the presence of Russian and OSCE officials. However, the ceasefire never took full hold, with particularly sharp fighting continuing around the Donetsk airport and in areas east of Mariupol, on the Sea of Azov. By the beginning of 2015, Russian/separatist forces had seized roughly 500 square kilometers of territory beyond the September 5 ceasefire line.

After a December lull, fighting accelerated again in January and early February 2015. At that time, NATO military officials estimated that 250-1,000 Russian military and military intelligence officers were in the occupied part of the Donbas, providing command and control and serving as advisors and trainers to the separatists as well as to "volunteers" from Russia. NATO officials believed that Russian personnel also operated the more sophisticated Russian military equipment. At that point, NATO did not believe that Russia had regular military units in Ukraine but noted that some 50,000 Russian troops had been deployed on the Russian side of the Ukraine-Russia border.

Ukrainian sources had a different estimate. They believed that Ukrainian forces faced a total of 36,000 Russian troops and separatist fighters in the Donbas. Of that total, the Ukrainians believed that 5,000-10,000 were Russian soldiers, though the bulk of the separatist fighters were Ukrainian citizens.

In February 2015, German Chancellor Angela Merkel and French President Francois Hollande brokered a settlement agreement between Ukrainian President Petro Poroshenko and Mr. Putin. That agreement—often referred to as the Minsk II accord—provided for a ceasefire, withdrawal of heavy weapons from the line of contact, and access for OSCE monitors to confirm the ceasefire and withdrawal. Minsk II also contained a number of additional measures designed to resolve the conflict and restore Ukrainian sovereignty over the Donbas, including withdrawal of all foreign forces, passage of a constitutional amendment on decentralization of political authority, an election law for the occupied region, a status law for the Donbas, and restoration of Ukrainian control of the full Ukraine-Russia border. The terms of Minsk II are clearly less favorable to Ukraine than the terms worked out in Minsk I in September 2014—in effect, a reward to the Kremlin for not observing the Minsk I agreement.

Minsk II got off to an inauspicious start. Russian and separatist forces launched a major assault on Ukrainian units in the Debaltsevo salient between the cities of Donetsk and Luhansk. They ratcheted down the fighting after capturing the territory but, as with the September 2014 ceasefire, the Minsk II ceasefire never really took hold—despite numerous subsequent attempts to negotiate a sustainable ceasefire.

A familiar pattern emerged over the next two years: shelling and fighting along the line of contact would flare up, followed by lulls and newly negotiated ceasefires, which never held and sometimes never even took effect. While both sides committed ceasefire violations, observers have attributed primary responsibility for violations to Russian/separatist forces.

As in the early days after the Crimean operation, Mr. Putin and the Kremlin deny there are any Russian military personnel in the Donbas—despite pictures of heavy weapons known only to be in the Russian inventory, the capture of Russian military personnel by Ukrainian forces, and the spotting by OSCE observers and Russian television of soldiers in Russian uniforms with Russian insignia. The Kremlin instead implausibly claims that all the separatist fighters are locals or "volunteers" from Russia.

NATO believes that the command structure for Russian/separatist forces in the occupied Donbas continues to consist of Russian military officers, while irregulars form the bulk of the armed personnel, though they have been and can be augmented by regular Russian army units if needed. The Ukrainian security service says that it has identified specific Russian military officers who occupy command positions in the forces of the so-called Donetsk and Luhansk "people's republics." The Ukrainian military and security service continue to believe that a larger portion of the fighters in the Donbas are active-duty Russian military personnel and that some are in organized Russian units.

Shelling and fighting continue along the line of contact in the Donbas. On most days, the Ukrainian military reports suffering killed and/or wounded in action.

The line of contact between Ukraine and the occupied part of the Donbas appears to be hardening. Leaders of the Donetsk and Luhansk "people's republics" have said that they will not permit a restoration of Ukrainian sovereignty—even though that is a central objective of Minsk II. The two statelets use the Russian ruble as their currency and have begun issuing passports, which the Russian government recognizes. On the other side, Ukraine has imposed a trade embargo on occupied Donbas and cut off the supply of electricity to the occupied part of Luhansk. This hardening of the line of contact will make it more difficult to achieve an eventual settlement.

The United States and European Union have regularly renewed sanctions on Russia and maintained a common line. Chancellor Merkel has repeatedly stated that full implementation of Minsk II is the prerequisite for easing sanctions, a position echoed by the Obama administration and, in its first months, by Trump administration officials.

What is Russia Seeking in Ukraine

By all appearances, the Kremlin is not implementing the Minsk II agreement and, at this point in time, apparently calculates that a simmering conflict in the Donbas better serves its interests. Such a conflict makes it more difficult for the government in Kyiv to pursue needed political and economic reforms or to implement the association agreement with the European Union. That is, it makes it harder for Ukraine to become a successful state and deepen links that will keep it out of a Russian sphere of influence.

Moscow is clearly unhappy about Western economic sanctions, yet it has eschewed steps that would lead to their easing. For example, it would not be difficult for the Kremlin to enforce a real ceasefire, given its control over Russian/separatist forces in the Donbas. It could also implement a withdrawal of heavy weapons away from the line of contact. If the Russians feared that the Ukrainian military might try to take advantage of the situation, they could visibly position additional Russian military units along the Russia-Ukraine border as a deterrent. Having implemented the ceasefire and withdrawal steps, OSCE monitors could then be invited to travel freely around the occupied part of the Donbas to confirm that the measures had been implemented.

Were the Kremlin to take these steps, the focus for implementation of Minsk II would shift to Kyiv. Political and public attitudes have understandably hardened over the past two years due to the continued fighting and casualties. The Ukrainian government could well find that it would have a difficult time implementing certain Minsk II provisions, such as the passage of a constitutional amendment on decentralization or an election law for the Donbas. If Ukraine could not deliver on those provisions, the stage would be set for Moscow to make a bid for the easing of sanctions on Russia.

Why has the Kremlin not taken such a step? The most plausible reason would appear to be that the Russians fear that Ukraine might be able to do its part to implement Minsk II. A settlement of the Donbas conflict at this point, however, does not appear to be a Kremlin objective. The Russian leadership instead sees advantages to maintaining a simmering conflict that it can use to put pressure on and destabilize the government in Kyiv.

The Russian leadership may have other reasons for holding to its present course. While Moscow was disappointed by election outcomes earlier this year in the Netherlands and France, Germany holds its elections in September. Polls indicate that Ms. Merkel remains the most popular politician, and her victory appears increasingly likely, but she is running for reelection for a fourth term at a time when many Western voters seek change. Ms. Merkel has provided the linchpin for European Union policy toward Russia and Ukraine, and the Russians no doubt would welcome her departure from office. That election gives Moscow an incentive to wait, in hopes that a change in Berlin might lead to a different German and European Union policy toward Russia—without Moscow doing anything to implement Minsk II.

The Role of OSCE

OSCE has played an important role in trying to resolve the conflict in the Donbas. The Trilateral Contact Group is headed by a special representative of the OSCE Chairperson-in-Office. In addition to OSCE, representatives of Ukraine and Russia are the other formal participants, and representatives of the Russian/separatist-occupied parts of Donetsk and Luhansk often take part. The Trilateral Contact Group has four working groups, which address political, security, humanitarian and economic questions. It has several times attempted to work out a true ceasefire, but with little success.

OSCE also provides a special monitoring mission, which is a civilian, unarmed mission that operates throughout Ukraine. The special monitoring mission currently has about 700 monitors. Many of them are deployed in eastern Ukraine, where the mission has been tasked with observing and reporting on the implementation of the Minsk II provisions on a ceasefire and withdrawal of heavy weapons from the line of contact. Unfortunately, the reports all too often document where Minsk II provisions are not observed. Still, the OSCE mission is important for the credibility of its observations, when there are often conflicting reports as to developments on the ground.

OSCE also maintains an observer mission at two checkpoints on the Russian border with occupied parts of the Donbas: Gukovo and Donetsk. While that presence allows reporting of what crosses from Russia into Ukraine (and vice-versa) at those two locations, there are many other border crossing points where Russian and separatist forces can cross freely without being observed by OSCE or other monitors on the ground.

Were Minsk II to be implemented, the special monitoring mission could expand its work and observe how additional Minsk II provisions were being implemented. OSCE also maintains a project coordinator in Kyiv to synchronize various OSCE activities aimed at promoting a variety of programs, including in the areas of constitutional, legal, human rights, media freedom, election and governance reforms.

The OSCE Permanent Council in Vienna provides a venue for the member states to exchange views on the Ukraine-Russia conflict and the situations in the Donbas and Crimea. Western delegations frequently use that forum to highlight where Russia or the separatists have violated Minsk II or OSCE commitments, such as to respect human rights. Such naming and shaming may not suffice to overcome Moscow's reluctance to implement Minsk II, but it serves to spotlight where the problem lies.

OSCE has not, however, been able to play a larger role in forcing a settlement to the ongoing conflict in the Donbas or the unsettled status of Crimea. That reflects the limitations of an organization that operates by consensus, in which Russia can block any OSCE effort with which it disagrees. For example, the Ukrainian government has in the past suggested that an armed OSCE police force might help to stabilize the situation in the Donbas, a proposal that has little chance of being developed given Russian opposition.

More broadly, Russia's aggression against Ukraine has weakened OSCE. One of the fundamental purposes of the organization is to promote a more peaceful, stable and secure Europe. Moscow's seizure of Crimea and actions in the Donbas undercut that goal and, unfortunately, make OSCE appear less effective as an organization.

U.S. and Western Policy

The United States and the West should continue to provide political support to Kyiv and, provided the Ukrainian government more effectively implements economic reforms and anti-corruption measures, additional economic assistance. It is also important that the United States continue to provide military assistance. This should include certain types of lethal assistance for the Ukrainian military, in particular man-portable anti-armor weapons, to increase the Ukrainians' capability to deal with the influx of Russian armor into the Donbas. The purpose of such assistance is not to give the Ukrainian military the ability to retake the Donbas. The military leadership in Kyiv understands that they cannot defeat the Russian army. The purpose of such assistance is to give the Ukrainians the ability to deny the Russian/separatist forces the ability to make easy gains, to deter further offensive actions, and to encourage the Kremlin to pursue a political settlement.

In parallel, U.S. and Western policy should aim to press Moscow to change its course in Ukraine and, as a matter of priority, work for a reasonable settlement in the Donbas. That is necessary to stop the fighting that has claimed some 10,000 lives.

The United States, European Union and other Western countries should continue to put political and economic pressure on the Kremlin. That means avoiding business as usual. When Mr. Putin observed the military parade in Red Square at Russia's VE Day commemoration on May 9, the only foreign leader to join him was the president of Moldova. That conveys to the Russian people a sense of the political isolation brought about by the Kremlin's policies. Mr. Putin clearly would like some normalization of the relationship with Washington. The Trump administration should make clear that Russia's aggression against Ukraine poses a major obstacle to such normalization.

Continuing to put pressure on the Kremlin also means maintaining the current economic and other sanctions that have been applied against Russia. To encourage Moscow to alter its course of maintaining a simmering conflict in the Donbas, the West should consider increased economic sanctions as well as an expansion of the number of Russian individuals targeted for visa bans and asset freezes; broadening visa bans to apply to family members could dramatically increase their impact. However, finding agreement on such steps could be difficult with the European Union, when some member states wish to return to business as usual with Moscow. It is also unclear if the Trump administration would favor additional sanctions. Congress should encourage the administration to do so.

In addition, it is important that the administration and NATO continue the steps agreed at last year's NATO summit in Warsaw to enhance the Alliance's conventional deterrence and defense capabilities in the Baltic region and Central Europe. Such steps will lead to more secure European allies who will be more confident in supporting Ukraine.The United States should also continue to support the German and French efforts to promote a solution to the Ukraine-Russia conflict. It is very difficult to see Minsk II being implemented, in large part due to Moscow's demonstrated disinterest. But Minsk II remains the only settlement process on the table, and Washington should encourage Kyiv to continue to engage. If Minsk II collapses—some might say when it collapses—it should be clear that Russia and the separatists bear full responsibility.

It is important to continue to engage Moscow. At the end of the day, Ukraine needs a settlement that has Russian buy-in. Otherwise, Moscow has too many levers that it can use to make life difficult for Kyiv and deny Ukraine a return to normalcy.

Finally, on Crimea. While one might envisage a settlement regarding the Donbas at some future point, it is all but impossible to imagine Mr. Putin or any future Russian leader agreeing to Crimea's return to Ukraine. At present, Kyiv lacks the political, economic and military leverage to change that. The Donbas fighting has been far more deadly, but the seizure of Crimea has been more destructive of the cardinal tenet of the Final Act: that states should not use military force to change borders or take territory from other countries. The United States and the West should not accept this. They should continue a policy of non-recognition of Crimea's illegal annexation and continue sanctions related to the peninsula until such time as Ukrainian sovereignty is restored or the Ukrainian government reaches some other settlement with Russia.

Conclusion

Mr. Chairman, Co-Chairman Smith, members of the Commission,

Over the past three years, Russia has employed military force to seize Crimea, and instigate and sustain a bloody armed conflict in the Donbas in pursuit of the Kremlin's goal of asserting a sphere of influence in the post-Soviet space and frustrating the ability of Ukrainians to realize their ambition of becoming a normal democratic European state.

These Russian actions are in stark violation of Russia's commitments under the Helsinki Final Act and other agreements, including the 1994 Budapest Memorandum on Security Assurances to Ukraine. These actions endanger peace and stability in Europe. Moreover, they raise concern that the Kremlin might be tempted to use force elsewhere in Europe.

The United States should work with its European partners to respond in a serious way. They should continue to provide Ukraine with political, economic and military support; maintain and intensify economic and other sanctions on Russia to induce a change in Kremlin policy; and keep open channels of communication for a settlement if Moscow alters its policy. This will require a sustained, patient effort. That is essential if we wish to realize the kind of Europe that was envisaged when the Final Act was signed in 1975.

○